LONDON'S
WATERSIDE WALKS

21 Walks Along the City's Most Captivating Rivers, Canals & Docks

Grand Union Canal, Westbourne Park

CITY BOOKS

City Books • Bath • England

First published 2019

Copyright © Survival Books 2019
Cover design: Herring Bone Design
Cover photo: Regent's Canal © Asiastock (Adobe Stock)
Maps © Jim Watson

City Books, c/o Survival Books Limited
Office 169, 3 Edgar Buildings
George Street, Bath BA1 2FJ, United Kingdom
+44 (0)1305-266918
info@survivalbooks.net
citybooks.co, survivalbooks.net and londons-secrets.com

British Library Cataloguing in Publication Data
A CIP record for this book is available
from the British Library

ISBN: 978-1-909282-96-4

Printed in China

Acknowledgements

The author would like to thank the many people who helped with research and provided information for this book. Special thanks are due to Gwen Simmonds for her invaluable research, Graeme & Louise Chesters and Richard Todd; Robbi Atilgan for editing; Susan Griffith for final proof checking; John Marshall for desktop publishing and photo selection; David Gillingwater for cover design; and the author's partner (Alexandra) for the constant supply of tea and coffee. Last, but not least, a special thank you to the many photographers – the unsung heroes – whose beautiful images bring London to life.

River Brent, Brentford

Author's Notes

Please note the following regarding the walks in this book.

♦ **Length & Duration:** The length of walks is approximate – shown to the nearest quarter mile – as is the time required to complete them, particularly if you make a lot of stops (coffee, lunch, museums, shopping, etc.). The average walking speed is around 3mph but we have allowed for a much slower pace of just 2mph. (The idea isn't to get from the start to finish as quickly as possible!) You can, of course, start a walk from either end, combine a number of walks to make a longer walk, or alternatively, shorten a walk. Most walks are graded easy or moderate with relatively few steep hills or steps.

♦ **Opening Hours:** Most of the buildings and public spaces (e.g. parks) included in the walks are open seven days a week; opening times may vary from weekdays to weekends and the season. Most parks and gardens offer free access, unless otherwise indicated. The opening hours of many sights and museums (etc.) are listed, though these are liable to change. Where there's an entry fee, it's noted.

♦ **Transport:** All walks start and end at or near a tube or railway station. Most can also be reached by bus (routes aren't listed as there are too many to include them all) and sometimes by river ferry. The postcode of the starting point is shown should you wish to drive. However, the nearest car park or on-road parking may be some distance away, particularly in central London – and can be expensive. Also, walks don't always return to the starting point.

♦ **Maps:** The maps aren't drawn to scale. Points of interest are numbered. An overall map of London is included on pages 8-9, showing the approximate location of walks.

♦ **Food & Drink:** Recommended 'pit stops' have been included in all walks – shown in **yellow** in the map key and in the text (other food and drink places are included as landmarks but aren't specifically recommended). When not listed, a pub/ restaurant's meal times are usually the 'standard' hours, e.g. noon-2.30 or 3pm and 6-11pm, although some are open all day and may also serve food all day (as do cafés). Many pubs are also open in the mornings for coffee and breakfast (etc.). Telephone numbers are listed where bookings are advisable or necessary, otherwise booking isn't usually required or even possible. Note that in the City of London (the financial district), many establishments are open only from Monday to Friday. A rough price guide is included (£ = inexpensive, ££ = moderate, £££ = expensive); most recommended places fall into the inexpensive category.

Contents

Beverley Brook

Introduction

London sits astride the celebrated River Thames, one of Europe's great rivers and the longest river in England, stretching 184 miles (296km) from its source in the Cotswold hills to the sea. Along the way the river navigates peaceful water meadows, unspoilt rural villages, and a wealth of historical towns and cities, before finally wending its way through the heart of London to end at the Thames Barrier in Greenwich. It's possible to walk the length of the river via the Thames Path, a national trail – indeed, eight of our walks include stretches of the Thames. The river provides a stunning backdrop to many of the city's top tourist attractions and has been witness to over 2,000 years of (recorded) history, as well as providing inspiration for generations of artists, musicians and writers.

The Thames once had many tributaries, some of which have ended up being buried in sewers, while others, like the Fleet, Tyburn and Walbrook, have been covered over and now run underground. However, some rivers escaped this fate – such as the Brent, the Lea and the Wandle – and continue to flow in the open to this day and feature in our walks. As well as rivers, the city is also awash with charming canals, including the Grand Union and Regent's Canals, former docks and other water features.

London's Waterside Walks explores 21 of the city's most captivating rivers, canals, docks and reservoirs. The walks are between 2¼ and 8½ miles in length, with the average around 5½ miles. However, it's best to allow half a day for the shorter walks and as much as a full day for the longer walks – particularly if you plan to partake of the many excellent pubs, restaurants and cafés along the routes (for your author, a good lunch is a prerequisite of a good walk!) – not to mention the many other diversions along the way. The aim is to take the 'scenic route', taking in as many interesting features as possible, rather than simply getting from A to B as fast as possible.

Writing *London's Waterside Walks* has been a fascinating and enjoyable journey of discovery. We hope that you enjoy these walks as much as we did; all you need is a comfortable pair of shoes, a sense of adventure – and this book!

David Hampshire
March 2019

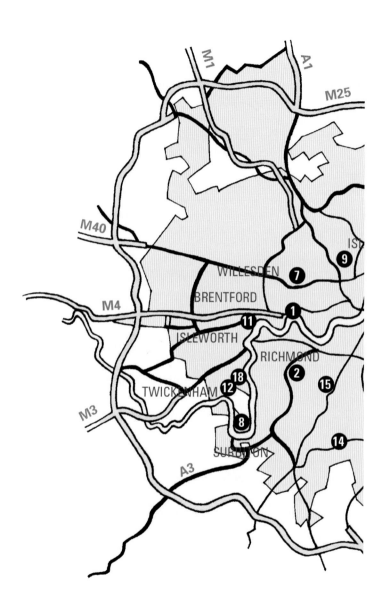

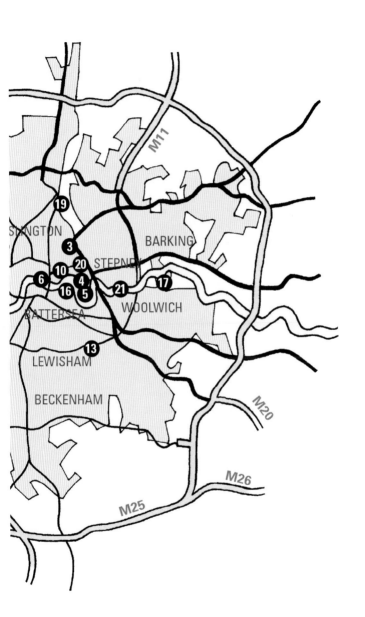

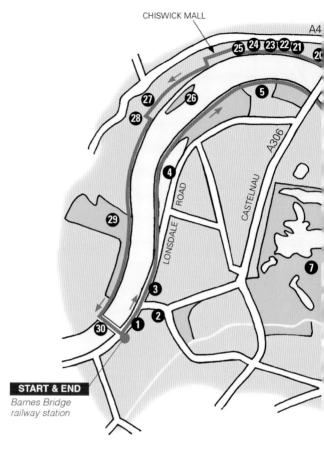

CHISWICK MALL

A4

1	The Terrace	11	Putney Bridge
2	Boathouse Café	12	St Mary's Church
3	Bull's Head	13	All Saints, Fulham
4	Leg o' Mutton Reservoir	14	Fulham Palace
5	St Paul's School	15	Bishop's Park
6	Hammersmith Bridge	16	Craven Cottage
7	London Wetland Centre	17	The Crabtree
8	Beverley Brook	18	The River Café
9	Leader's Gardens	19	The Blue Boat
10	Duke's Head	20	The Blue Anchor

START & END
Barnes Bridge
railway station

● Places of Interest   ○ Food & Drink

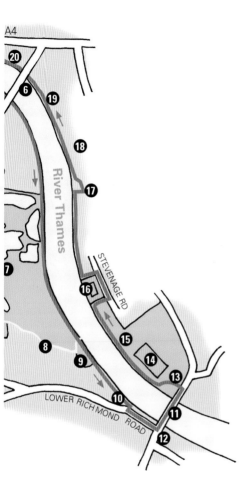

Barnes to Putney

WALK 1

Distance: 8 miles (13 km)
Terrain: easy
Duration: 4 hours
Start/End: Barnes Bridge rail
Postcode: SW13 0NP

BARNES TO PUTNEY

This walk takes you along a scenic section of the Thames Path – the long-distance National Trail footpath running along the banks of the River Thames – from Barnes Railway Bridge to Putney Bridge and back again. This stretch of the river is a sporting mecca, home to a plethora of rowing clubs and the venue of the annual University Boat Race (between crews from Cambridge and Oxford) that starts at Putney Bridge and ends at Chiswick Bridge. Our route includes some of London's most coveted residential areas, not least affluent Barnes and fashionable Chiswick, with their splendid Thameside mansions and village atmosphere. We also take in the former working-class areas of Fulham – with an industrial history dating back to the 15th century – and Hammersmith.

Highlights include Barnes village, the Leg o' Mutton Reservoir, St Paul's School, the London Wetland Centre, Putney Bridge, Fulham Palace, Hammersmith Bridge, beautiful Chiswick Mall and its elegant Georgian architecture, and a wealth of lovely gardens, parks and historic riverside inns.

The Terrace, Barnes

Start Walking...

Exit Barnes Bridge railway station and cross over **The Terrace** ❶, a handsome street lined with pastel-coloured Georgian houses overlooking a peaceful stretch of the Thames. Head right along the Thames Path, away from the bridge, and after a few hundred metres you reach the junction with Barnes High Street – if you need a caffeine boost, visit the **Boathouse Café** ❷ , some 200m along the High Street on the right. Just past the junction is the **Bull's Head** ❸ pub, one of London's premier jazz venues for the last 60 years. It does a good brunch from 11am (noon at weekends) and a tasty Sunday roast.

Keep walking north along Lonsdale Road and follow the Thames Path as it curves along the western edge of the intriguingly-named Small Profit Dock Gardens, an urban meadow that surrounds the **Leg o' Mutton Reservoir** ❹ (aka Lonsdale Road Reservoir). The reservoir was constructed in 1838 by Thames Water and has a capacity of 260,000m³, although it was decommissioned in 1960. It was designated a Local Nature Reserve in 1990; covering some 20 acres/8ha, the reserve is managed by Richmond Council and is home to an abundance of birdlife, including cormorants, herons and common terns. Just after the reserve you pass the Swedish School, founded in 1907 and located in Barnes since 1976, while some 400m further on you come to an altogether more famous seat of learning, **St Paul's School** ❺ (see box).

A short way after St Paul's School, the Thames follows a loop south beneath beautiful **Hammersmith Bridge** ❻. This Grade II* listed suspension bridge was designed by Sir Joseph Bazalgette – who

built London's sewerage system – and opened in 1887, replacing an earlier bridge constructed in 1827. Two failed attempts to destroy the bridge were made by the Irish Republican Army (IRA) in 1939 and 2000.

Beverley Brook

Continuing south, the Thames Path runs alongside the **London Wetland Centre** ❼ (see box on page 14), an unexpected urban wildlife oasis. A little way past the Wetland Centre you cross over the **Beverley Brook** ❽ (see **Walk 2**) where it flows into the Thames, and arrive at Putney Embankment (a conservation area) and **Leader's Gardens** 🟡, a popular riverside park with a play area and café. The park is the start of the unique Putney Sculpture Trail (2008), which features nine near life-sized figurative sculptures donated by sculptor Alan Thornhill positioned along the south side of the Thames on either side of Putney Bridge. Soon after Leader's Gardens you pass a cluster of rowing clubs and their handsome boathouses, which include the London Rowing Club, founded in 1856.

WWT London Wetland Centre

The London Wetland Centre (entrance fee) covers an area of over 100 acres (40ha), an unexpectedly large wildlife habitat close to central London, and Europe's best urban wildlife viewing area. The centre was created by the Wildfowl and Wetlands Trust (WWT) and is based on four concrete reservoirs which became redundant after the completion of the Thames Water Ring Main in the '90s. It took five years to establish the centre – during which time 300,000 plants and 27,000 trees were planted – which opened in May 2000. For more information see wwt.org.uk/wetland-centres/london.

London Wetland Centre

From here, the path leads past some handsome Victorian terraced houses and the 150-year-old **Duke's Head** 🔟 pub on the corner of Thames Place. A boathouse-style pub, occupying a Grade II listed building, it's a good choice for lunch. A bit further along Putney Embankment is another popular Victorian pub, the Star and Garter, closely followed by Thai Square Putney Bridge restaurant. Soon after the restaurant (just before Waterman's Green) bear right onto Lower Richmond Road, then go left across **Putney Bridge** ⓫. Like Hammersmith Bridge, it was designed by Sir Joseph Bazalgette and was constructed in 1884. It's now best known as the starting point for the annual University Boat Race. On the opposite side of the bridge approach is **St Mary's Church** ⓬ (Grade II* listed), parts of which date from the 15th century.

All Saints, Fulham

On the north side of Putney Bridge descend the stairs on the left, adjacent to a bus shelter. On the right is **All Saints, Fulham** ⓭, which has a Kentish ragstone church tower dating from 1440 – a local landmark. The rest of the church is Victorian, designed by Sir Arthur Blomfield in Gothic Perpendicular style, although the interior contains many fine monuments from the old (pre-Victorian) church. Take the path to the left leading to the Thames Embankment and head northwest past Pryor's Bank Gardens and ancient **Fulham Palace** ⓮ (see box opposite).

Fulham Palace

A residence of the Bishops of London from around 700 AD, Fulham Palace (Grade I listed) was their country home from at least the 11th century and their main residence from the early 20th century until 1973 (when they moved to Dean's Court, near St Paul's Cathedral in the City). The current building consists of a Tudor manor house, dating from the reign of Henry VII (1485-1509) – said to be haunted by the ghosts of Protestant heretics who were persecuted in the great hall – with Georgian additions and a Victorian chapel (see fulhampalace.org for information).

Just past the palace is **Bishop's Park** 15, which opened in 1893 and contains tennis courts, bowling greens, a clubhouse, playgrounds, a lake and unique urban beach, plus a café. Continue along the shady Thames Path to the end, where you need to cross Bishop's Park (Fielder's Meadow) to Stevenage Road to circumnavigate **Craven Cottage** 16 football ground. The home of Fulham Football Club since 1896, the club was founded in 1879 and is the oldest-established London football club to play in the Premier League.

Just past the Cottage take the path on the left across Stevenage Park to return to the Thames Path. Turn right and for the next 400m, you pass several housing estates and then Rowberry Mead, a small local park, before turning inland and down some steps to The Foundry. Turn left past **The Crabtree** 17, a Victorian gastropub with a pretty orchard beer garden, and left along the passage beside the garden to continue along the Thames Path. A few steps along you pass the Dorset Wharf Community Hall and 200m further on come to **The River Café** 18, Ruth Rogers' (and the late Rose Gray's) legendary Italian restaurant on the site of the former Thames Wharf. Further along is another fine hostelry, **The Blue Boat** 19, which has a patio garden with panoramic views. From here the path passes under Hammersmith Bridge, which you encountered earlier, before continuing along Lower Mall where there's another historic riverside inn, **The Blue Anchor** 20, dating back to the early 18th century.

The first green space you reach is **Furnivall Gardens** 21 (named after the scholar Dr Frederick James Furnivall) – once the location of the mouth of Hammersmith Creek – just after which the path turns inland and then left to the tiny **Dove** 22 pub, which used to be a coffee house but is now a quintessential English pub. Charles II and Nell Gwyn allegedly had assignations here and it has reportedly inspired writers and musicians. In 1740, the poet James

The Dove

Thomson is said to have written *Rule Britannia* in an upstairs room, while Gustav

The Blue Anchor

Holst used to compose music here – it must be something in the beer! From the pub continue along the Upper Mall to number 26: the handsome Georgian mansion, **Kelmscott House** ㉓ (see box). This was the former home of artist, designer and man-for-all-seasons, William Morris (1834-1896), who lived here from 1879 until his death.

A few hundred metres further along is **Linden House** ㉔, a grand brick building dating from 1733 with an entrance flanked by Ionic columns; it's been home to the London Corinthian Sailing Club (founded 1894) since 1963. Continue along the Thames Path through an arch and, just before the Upper Mall Open Space, you come to yet another handsome pub, the **Old Ship** ㉕, dating from 1722. After the open space the path leads right, then left into Hammersmith Terrace; look for number 7, the former home of Emery Walker (1851-1933), engraver, photographer and

Fuller's Brewery

printer. Hammersmith Terrace leads into Chiswick Mall, which is lined with large, attractive, mainly 18th-century houses, some of which are separated from their riverside gardens by the road! Some 200m along the Mall you pass **Chiswick Eyot** ㉖, an uninhabited island (3.3acres/1.3ha) in the Thames that can be reached on foot at low tide. Just past the eyot is **Fuller's Brewery** ㉗ (tours can be booked), which dates from 1845, although beer has been brewed in Chiswick for over 350 years.

At the end of Chiswick Mall the road swings right into Church Street past **St Nicholas Church** ㉘ (see box opposite), where the old village of Chiswick was established. St Nicholas is the patron saint of fishermen and sailors, among others, which is appropriate as Chiswick began life as a fishing village. Take the left-hand walkway next to the small wharf and continue along the Thames Path to the Chiswick Lifeboat Station. From here, if time allows, you can take a detour some 400m inland, via Corney Reach Way and Grantham Road, to visit splendid Chiswick House & Gardens. A few hundred metres further on you pass **Duke's Meadow** ㉙ – owned by the Duke of Devonshire until 1923 – and the King's House Sports Grounds, before arriving back at **Barnes Railway Bridge** ㉚. The Grade II listed bridge dates from 1895 – the original bridge, constructed in 1849, still stands on the upstream side – and has an adjacent footbridge leading to the railway station, which marks the end of the walk.

Kelmscott House

William Morris' last London home was built in around 1780 and was originally called The Retreat. Morris renamed it after his Oxfordshire home, Kelmscott Manor, and occasionally travelled between the two by boat – those were the days! Today, the William Morris Society occupies the coach house and basement rooms, and curates a small but interesting museum (Thu and Sat, 2-5pm) with a collection of Morris designs and memorabilia.

St Nicholas Church

Built in the Perpendicular style with a ragstone tower dating from 1446 – the only reminder of the medieval church – St Nicholas was rebuilt in 1882 by John Loughborough Pearson, one of Britain's leading Victorian architects. William Hogarth (1697-1764), fellow artist James McNeill Whistler (1834-1903) and architect William Kent (1685-1748) are buried in the churchyard.

Food & Drink

(2) Boathouse Café: At 4 Barnes High Street, the Boathouse is the ideal place to get your morning caffeine fix (8am-5pm, Sun 9am-5pm, £).

(10) Duke's Head: Grand Victorian pub on Putney Embankment serving tasty food, with a small terrace overlooking the Thames (noon-11pm, midnight Thu-Sat, £-££).

(17) The Crabtree: Iconic gastropub on a quiet stretch of the Thames between Hammersmith and Putney bridges with a pretty garden (Mon-Sat noon-11pm, Sun noon-10.30pm, £-££).

Barnes Railway Bridge

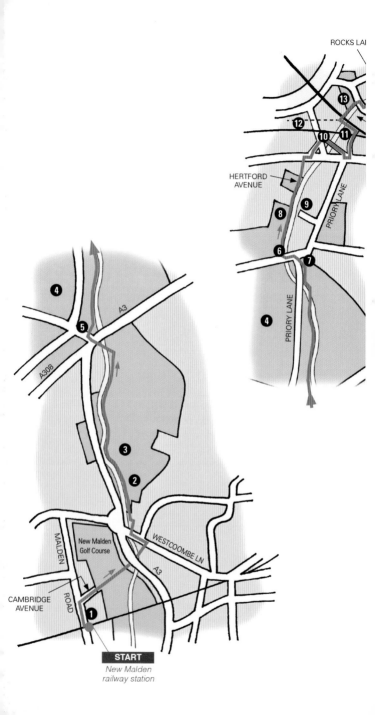

ROCKS LANE

13

12

10 **11**

HERTFORD
AVENUE

9

8

PRIORY LANE

6

7

4

PRIORY LANE

4

A3

5

A308

3

2

WESTCOOMBE LN

MALDEN

New Malden
Golf Course

A3

CAMBRIDGE
AVENUE

ROAD

1

START
New Malden
railway station

Beverley Brook

WALK 2

Distance: 8½ miles (13½ km)
Terrain: easy
Duration: 4 hours
Start: New Malden rail
End: Putney Bridge tube
Postcode: KT3 4PX

BEVERLEY BROOK

This walk follows the course of Beverley Brook (9 miles/14½ km), one of only a handful of tributaries of the River Thames that hasn't been buried underground. The brook rises in Worcester Park (Surrey) – where it runs through a culvert for its first few miles – and flows into the Thames to the north of Putney Embankment at Barn Elms. The walk is waymarked, although you need to take care as there are a number of junctions where the signage is missing or ambiguous.

The brook derives its name from the European beaver, which became extinct in Britain in the 16th century. For much of the 20th century, Beverley Brook was the depository for poorly treated sewage from sewage works in Worcester Park. However, the redirection of sewage pipes and improved treatment methods (coupled with on-going regeneration) have dramatically improved water quality, and increased the variety of fish and other wildlife in the river. Today, the brook is a (mostly) peaceful oasis offering a surprisingly varied and beautiful walk through some of south London's most attractive countryside.

We join the river in New Malden and follow it across Wimbledon Common and Richmond Park – one of the brook's most beautiful and tranquil stretches – to Roehampton and Barnes, where it runs along the fringes of Barnes Green and Barnes Common, before emptying into the Thames just north of Putney Bridge.

Beverley Brook

Start Walking…

Exit New Malden railway station (mainline trains from Waterloo station) and go right on Coombe Road. You're in the heart of the village here and there are a number of options for coffee or breakfast, including the **Village Café 1** , a few steps up on the right. Continue along Coombe Road and take the second right onto Cambridge Avenue. It begins as a suburban road, lined with mock Tudor houses, but after 500m or so it becomes a dirt track and cuts across New Malden Golf Course, before the tarmac reappears just before the A3/Kingston Bypass. There's an underpass under the A3 and you re-join the footpath between two mock Tudor houses – look for the blue sign to Raynes Park and Wimbledon – where you get your first glimpse of Beverley Brook as it flows beneath your feet as you emerge on to Westcoombe Avenue. The water is clear and abundant with fish; such a shame it isn't like this along the entire length of its course.

Turn left onto Westcoombe Avenue and walk to the junction with Coombe Lane, where you go left. Cross over the road (there's a zebra crossing) and turn right on Beverley Avenue and continue to the end of the road and go left along the narrow path (signposted Robin Hood Gate) that runs along the edge of **Beverley Meads Recreation Ground 2**. Around 50m along the path you're reunited with Beverley Brook, which you now follow north through Beverley Meads and **Fishponds Wood Nature Reserve 3**, an area of woodland and fields that's part of Wimbledon Common (see box). The wood was once part of the Abbey of Merton before

Wimbledon Common

Wimbledon Common, together with Putney Heath and Putney Lower Common, is the largest expanse of heathland (1,136 acres/460ha) in London. Created in 1871 by an Act of Parliament for public recreation and the preservation of flora and fauna, the common provides an oasis of calm in the midst of urban southwest London. The common is a popular recreational area, not least for walkers, runners, cyclists and horse riders (with 16mi/26km of bridleways), plus an 18-hole golf course, cricket pitches and 48 acres (20ha) of playing fields. It's also famous in literature (and on television) as the home to Elizabeth Beresford's furry rubbish recyclers, the Wombles.

it was demolished in the 16th century during the dissolution of the monasteries. In more recent times the land became

Fishponds Wood Nature Reserve

Walk 2

Beverley Brook, Richmond Park

wooded (mostly oak and birch) and was part of an adjacent farm until shortly after the Second World War, when the council became the landowner. The area is a Site of Special Scientific Interest (SSSI), noted for its water-loving plants, butterflies, dragonflies, damselflies, frogs and newts, all of which are abundant in the spring and summer months. You may also see

---

Richmond Park

Richmond Park is the largest royal park in London and the second-largest urban park in Europe, extending to 2,360 acres (955ha). The park is classified as a European Special Area of Conservation, a National Nature Reserve and a Site of Special Scientific Interest, with a plethora of flora and fauna. The oldest, largest and most widespread inhabitants of the park – its trees and, especially, its oaks – provide homes for a wide range of wildlife, from ants and beetles to birds and bats. However, its most visible residents are red and fallow deer (numbering around 650), which roam freely within much of the park. It's also an important refuge for squirrels, rabbits, foxes, shrews, mice, voles, cardinal click and stag beetles, plus numerous varieties of fungi. Birdlife is hugely varied, with some 150 species recorded (over 60 breed here), including all three native woodpeckers, kestrels, owls and a variety of waterfowl.

---

kingfishers and mandarin ducks here, while the sparkling brook is alive with sticklebacks, roach and chubb.

After around 1½ km you reach the northern edge of Wimbledon Common, where the path goes left over a brick bridge (just before a sports pavilion) to the busy A3 road which separates the common from Richmond Park; the last few hundred metres of the path overlap with the Capital Ring path around London. Cross the A3 via the pedestrian crossing on Kingston Vale and enter **Richmond Park** ❹ (see box) through **Robin Hood Gate** ❺ . Take the right-hand path (around the car park) that loops back to the western bank of the Beverley Brook and continues north. The brook's route through the park is one of the loveliest sections of the waterway, although there may be some disturbance as it's being restored and re-naturalised (restoring natural habitats) to meet environmental targets. After one and a half kilometres the path crosses the brook over a wooden footbridge and veers away from

Roehampton Gate Café

Barnes Green

A delightful spot with a large pond, Barnes Green is the venue for several open-air events – including Barnes Fair in July and the Barnes Food Fair in September – and regular covered markets. In former times the stocks were located here and during medieval fairs there were races around the pond. Today, it's a popular venue for ball games, picnics and feeding the ducks, and is home to the Barnes Green Social Centre, the Old Sorting Office Arts Centre and Barnes Methodist Church (1906). There are some nice places to stop for refreshments around the green.

the brook to follow Priory Lane north to **Roehampton Gate** ❻. If you need sustenance, the **Roehampton Gate Café** ❼ – run by the celebrated Colicci family – is a good place to stop.

Exit the park and turn left just after Roehampton Gate Lodge to follow the narrow path running along the outside of the park wall; the byway leads to a bridge over Beverley Brook and swings right to run alongside the brook. This peaceful trail takes you across **Palewell Common** ❽, where there are playing fields on your left, followed by the **Bank of England Sports Centre** ❾ and the National Tennis Centre on your right. The path bears left through some allotments and ends on Hertford Avenue, where you turn right and follow the road some 500m to the end, turning right again onto

Upper Richmond Road. Cross the road at the first pedestrian crossing and walk 100m to take a detour left along Priests Bridge. Follow the road round to **The Stag's Head Barnes** ❿, a boutique pub with a red-brick and mock Tudor façade. Beverley Brook can be spotted again as it flows under a bridge next to the pub and off between the elegant back gardens of Barnes. Meanwhile, you return to Upper Richmond Road at the end of Priests Bridge, turn left and take the second left into Vine Road.

Continue over the first of two level crossings and turn left to **Vine Road Recreation Ground** ⓫, then follow the path along its northern edge until it crosses over Beverley Book and some 50m further along does a 90-degree right turn to join the **Beverley Path** ⓬, an ancient route between Mortlake and Putney. After around 150m the path emerges onto Willow Avenue, which leads to Station Road with the brook running alongside. Cross Station Road and take the path to the right of the bridge to continue following the brook as it skirts the eastern edge of **Barnes Green** ⓭ (see box).

After a short distance the brook disappears into a culvert and the path swings away to the right across **Barnes Common** ⓮. Extending to some 124 acres (50ha), Barnes Common is one of the largest areas of unenclosed common land within easy reach of central London.

Palewell Common

WWT London Wetland Centre

It's been owned by the church since the Middle Ages and is now managed by the borough of Richmond-upon-Thames. Once an expanse of marshland, it was drained in the late 19th century and now comprises open grassland, trees and woodland. Designated a Local Nature Reserve, it's home to an abundance of flora and fauna, including the burnet rose and speckled wood butterfly, and is noted for its grasses, but is too open to support many mammals. The path leads to Rocks Lane where you cross over and carry on ahead, bearing right past the **Rocks Lane Multi Sport Centre** 15 on your left, and then head south past **Barnes Old Cemetery** 16 (see box) on Putney Lower Common.

Head east from the cemetery until you come to a path going north, which leads to a small bridge over Beverley Brook. Just north of here is **Barn Elms Playing Fields** 17, named for a manor house once owned by Sir Francis Walsingham – Elizabeth I's spymaster – and later the Hoare banking family. To the north of Barn Elms is the **WWT London Wetland Centre** 18, Europe's best urban wildlife-viewing area. Turn right over the bridge and follow the tree-lined path along the north bank of the brook to its final destination where it flows into the Thames via a weir; the brook ends in a tired trickle rather than a triumphant torrent – a sad end for such a pretty waterway.

You're now on the Thames Path, where you turn right on Putney Embankment in the direction of Putney Bridge. This

Barnes Old Cemetery

A number of distinguished Victorians are buried in Barnes Old Cemetery, established in 1854 as an additional burial ground for Barnes parish churchyard. The cemetery closed in the '50s and Richmond Council acquired it in 1966 with the intention of turning it into a lawn cemetery, although the plans were later abandoned. It's now one of London's forgotten cemeteries, overgrown with trees and shrubs, with many of the monuments vandalised and statues decapitated. It's a sorry sight, but it's also an atmospheric and evocative place with an air of quiet seclusion. (There's another historic cemetery – Putney Lower Common Cemetery – in the southeast corner of the common.)

Barnes Old Cemetery

Food & Drink

1 **Village Café:** Close to New Malden station and handy for coffee or a bacon butty (Mon-Fri 6am-4pm, Sat-Sun 9am-3pm, £).

7 **Roehampton Gate Café:** The Italian influence guarantees excellent coffee, tasty cakes and authentic stone-baked pizza (8am-5.30pm, winter 4pm, £).

19 **The Rocket:** JD Wetherspoon pub near Putney Bridge, offering beer, burgers and brilliant river views (8am-11pm, Sun until 10.30pm, £).

stretch of the river is home to a profusion of superb riverside pubs where you can toast your completion of the walk. These include the Duke's Head around 300m before the bridge; **The Rocket 19** at the foot of Putney Wharf Tower (a '60s office block); and The Boathouse, a striking modern pub with a waterfront beer garden and balcony. The latter two are just past **St Mary's Church 20** , south of the bridge.

From the church follow the riverside path past the Boathouse and Carluccio's around to the right and go left on Deodar Road. Around 100m along on the left there are steps leading up to **Fulham Railway Bridge 21** which incorporates a footbridge that allows for a scenic stroll across the Thames. From here it's straight ahead to Putney Bridge tube station – and the end of the walk.

Fulham Railway Bridge

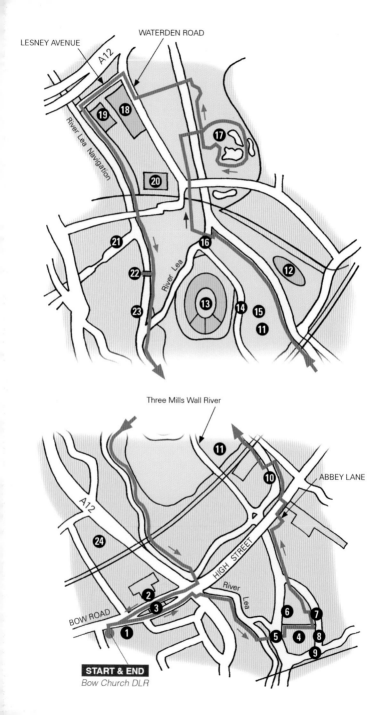

LESNEY AVENUE

WATERDEN ROAD

A12

River Lea Navigation

19   18

20

21

22

23

River Lea

16

17

12

13   14   15
          11

Three Mills Wall River

11

10

ABBEY LANE

A12

24

HIGH STREET

River Lea

2

3

6   7

5   4   8
        9

1

BOW ROAD

START & END
Bow Church DLR

● Places of Interest   ● Food & Drink

WALK 3

Bow Back Rivers & River Lea

Walk 3

Distance: 5½ miles (9 km)
Terrain: easy
Duration: 3 hours
Start/End: Bow Church DLR
Postcode: E3 3AA

The Bow Back Rivers is the name for a complex of waterways between Bow and Stratford in East London, which connect the River Lea (also written as 'Lee') to the Thames via Bow Creek. Some 10 miles (16km) in length, they flow across Stratford Marshes and are thought to date back at least to the time of Alfred the Great, who cut a channel here in 896 to strand a band of Danish invaders. Since the 12th century, efforts have been made to drain the marshes and a number of waterways were constructed to power watermills. These included Bow Back River, Channelsea River, City Mill River, Prescott Channel, Pudding Mill River, Three Mills Back River, Three Mills Wall River and Waterworks River, many of which still exist.

The River Lea originates in Leagrave near Luton in the Chiltern Hills and flows generally southeast through East London to join the Bow Creek tidal estuary. It's one of the largest rivers in London and the easternmost major tributary of the Thames. Much of the river has been canalised to provide a navigable route for boats (confusingly named the Lee Navigation) and the upper reaches of the Lea have been a major source of drinking water for London since 1613, when an artificial waterway – the New River – was constructed to bring water to the capital.

Our walk begins in Bow Road in East London and heads east to join the River Lea, which we follow it to Three Mills Island. From here we head north along the Waterworks River to the Queen Elizabeth Olympic Park, along the City Mills River and the River Lea to the Wetlands Walk, before returning via the Lee Navigation and River Lea to Bow.

Three Mills Island

Start Walking...

From Bow Church DLR station follow Bow Road east, passing **The Bow Bells** 1 pub – a traditional East End boozer serving good food – or, if you fancy a coffee, the **Nunnery Café** 2 at the Nunnery Gallery (181 Bow Road) is a good choice. Just across from the gallery is **St Mary's Bow Church** 3 (Grade II listed), located on an island in the middle of the road. A church has stood here for 700 years; the present building – constructed of Kentish ragstone with brick additions – is thought to have a 14th-century structure, the tower being added in the 15th century.

Continue along Bow Road and the High Street to Bow Roundabout, where you cross over the A12; the crossing brings you to a footpath which leads down to the River Lea. Turn right to walk

St Mary's Bow Church

beside the river and after around 400m, turn left on Three Mill Lane to cross the river to **Three Mills Island** 4 (see box). Just along on the left is the **House Mill** 5 , the world's largest tidal mill still in existence and now a museum (for information and opening times, see housemill.org.uk). The House Mill (Grade I listed) was built in 1776 by Daniel Bisson between two houses once occupied by the miller's family. Just across the cobbles

Three Mills Island

Known as Three Mills since medieval times, the site was originally part of an abbey destroyed during Henry VIII's dissolution of the monasteries in the 1530s. There were believed to have been eight or nine mills operating on the River Lea at the time of the *Domesday Book* (1086), providing flour for the bakers of Stratford-atte-Bow (modern Bow), who in turn supplied bread to the City of London. They were later used to grind grain to fuel Londoners' demand for gin. In 1728, Three Mills was purchased by Peter Lefevre, a Huguenot, ensuring its survival to the 20th century.

is Clock Mill, which was rebuilt in 1817 and operated until 1952; it's now part of the Three Mills Film Studio, former home of the reality TV show *Big Brother*. The third mill has long disappeared.

Turn left opposite the Clock Mill alongside Three Mills Wall River, which is lined with resident narrowboats, and cross the junction to see the **Helping Hands Memorial** 6 (see box on page 30) on the edge of the circular Three Mills Green.

House Mill

Helping Hands Memorial

This poignant memorial by Alec Peever was unveiled in 2001 and commemorates the centenary of a tragedy that took place here on July 12th 1901. Four men lost their lives in a well after being overcome by carbon dioxide fumes; ironically, three died while trying to save the first victim, Thomas Pickett. One of the would-be rescuers was Godfrey Maule Nicholson, managing director of the Nicholson Gin Distillery and owner of the Three Mills site.

Return to Three Mill Lane, turn left and go straight ahead to **Three Mills Lock** ❼, aka Prescott Lock, opened in 2009 on the **Prescott Channel** ❽. The channel was built in 1930-35 as part of a flood relief scheme for the Lee Navigation (see below), and the lock, which opened in 2009, includes a sluice structure to control water levels in the Bow Back Rivers, thus making navigation easier. To the south, the channel flows into the **Channelsea River** ❾, a tidal river that empties into Bow Creek, part of the River Lea. From the lock, head north along the Prescott Channel to the top of Three Mills Island, where a bridge in the northwest corner crosses the channel with the Three Mills Wall River on your left. To the east is the magnificent Abbey Mills Pumping Station (Grade II* listed), a sewage pumping station designed by Sir Joseph Bazalgette and built in 1865-8, housing eight beam engines. It was replaced by a modern pumping station in 1997, located 200m south of the original station.

Cross the bridge and continue north alongside the river to the High Street. Turn right and cross over just past the Abbey Lane Open Space and Greenway footpath to access the Waterworks River footpath. The **Waterworks River** ❿ is an artificial channel which was cut for the Stratford Waterworks in 1743, and is another of the Bow Back Rivers that flow into Bow Creek. Walk along the river to Bridgewater Road, cross over the bridge to the western side and take the path north to the **Queen Elizabeth Olympic Park** ⓫ (see box opposite). On the eastern bank is the sinuous **London Aquatics Centre** ⓬, designed by architect Zaha Hadid in 2004; it's now a public swimming pool (entrance fee, 6am-10.30pm).

Over to the left, the view is dominated by the iconic **London Stadium** ⓭, now home to West Ham United FC. It's open for tours most days (10am-3pm, fee – see stadiumtourbookings. london-stadium.com/

Queen Elizabeth Olympic Park

booking/default.htm). Just to the east of the stadium is another waterway, the **City Mill River** ⓮, which formerly fed City Mill, used for the production of chemicals in the late 19th and early 20th centuries. Midway between the two rivers is the **ArcelorMittal Orbit** ⓯ (fee, Mon-Fri 11am-5pm, Sat-Sun 10am-6pm), a 376ft (115m) sculpture and observation tower – incorporating the world's longest tunnel slide – designed by Sir Anish Kapoor and Cecil Balmond of engineering group Arup.

Queen Elizabeth Olympic Park

Built for the 2012 Summer Olympics and Paralympics, the Olympic Park (renamed in honour of Queen Elizabeth's Diamond Jubilee the same year) contains several major sporting venues, including the London Stadium, the Lea Valley VeloPark and the London Aquatics Centre. There are 111 acres (45ha) of open space in the park, including gardens, broad meadows and intricate wetlands. See queenelizabetholympicpark.co.uk for information.

Continue for around 200m past the Aquatics Centre and Stratford Walk (which crosses over the Waterworks River) along the western edge of the river to where it joins the River Lea just north of **Carpenters Road Lock** ⓰. The rising radial lock was built in 1933-4 to stem flooding in the Lower Lea Valley and was recently restored and opened to river

Carpenters Road Lock

traffic. Cross the River Lea and go straight ahead to London Way – one of the park's main thoroughfares – where you go right, passing over Carpenters Road and Waterden Road. After around 100m, take the path to the right over the footbridge to access **Wetlands Walk** ⓱.

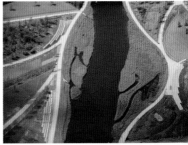
Olympic Park, Wetlands

The Wetlands is an area of ponds and lakes rich in plant and wildlife. Go right and follow the path around the wetlands in a figure of eight, before returning to where you started. Over to the right is the East Village housing development, formerly the athletes' Olympic Village; waste water from the estate is cleaned and treated in the wetlands. Continue north along the River Lea, passing the Timber Lodge Café and Tumbling Bay Playground over to the right, and cross back over the River Lea via the bridge to Waterden Road and **Here East** ⓲ (see box on page 32), located in the former press and broadcasting centre of the London Olympic Games. Follow the road north past Here East to Lesney Avenue, which leads to the Lee Navigation, so-called because much of the natural River Lea has been canalised in order to provide a navigable route.

Opposite the river is **Canalside** ⓳, a retail centre with numerous places to meet, eat, shop and relax, overlooking the riverside gardens – it's the ideal spot for a snack or lunch. Continue along the canalside path, which here is part of the Capital Ring route, passing the **Copper Box Arena** ⑳ (7am-10pm) on the left; a venue for handball and fencing during the Olympics that's now a leisure centre (see copperboxarena.org.uk). Over the river on the right is Hackney Wick railway station. The path continues past the East London Energy Visitors Centre, under White Post Lane and past the Milk Float, a narrowboat converted into a café (open Thu 6-11pm and weekends 10am-6pm). On the right is the junction with the **Hertford Union Canal** ㉑, opened in 1831, which links the Lee Navigation with Regent's Canal 1.25mi (2km) to the west.

Old Ford Locks

Continuing south on the Capital Ring you soon come to the Monier Road Footbridge, which provides access to the **Stour Space Gallery** ㉒ on the opposite bank, a huge ramshackle community arts centre with a licensed café and lovely terrace. A few hundred metres further is **Old Ford Locks** ㉓, a paired lock and weir. This part of the Lee Navigation is called the Hackney Cut, an artificial channel built in the 18th century to cut off

a large loop in the natural river. The old lock-keeper's cottages here have been converted into a single house and for ten years were used for filming Channel 4's early morning show, *The Big Breakfast*.

Just past the lock the path crosses a footbridge over the natural River Lea, which re-joins the Lee Navigation at this point. Follow the River Lea along the edge of the park, crossing under the Greenway path (marked by vast pipes) where it goes over the Lea. Just past the end of the park, over to the right (on the opposite side of the A12) is the **Bow Quarter** ㉔, a gated community of flats and cottages occupying the former Bryant & May match factory that closed in 1979. A little further along, the river hugs the A12, where you arrive back at the Bow Roundabout and the Bow Back River. Leave the river here and turn right to go back along the High Street to Bow Street DLR station – and the end of the walk. If you fancy a drink or something to eat, the **Bow Bells** ❶ pub a few hundred metres before the station is a good choice.

Here East

An innovative hi-tech centre for business, tech, media, education and data, Here East was designed as a hub for new entrepreneurs to co-exist and collaborate with global, established businesses and to support product innovation. Spread over 1.2 million sq ft (111,000 sq metres), it builds on the creative heritage of Hackney Wick, providing a thriving commercial space and creating over 7,500 jobs on site and in the local community.

Food & Drink

(2) **Nunnery Café:** Café in the Nunnery Gallery (housed in a former 19th-century convent) on Bow Road, serving artisan food and good coffee (Tue-Sun, 10am-4.30pm, closed Mon, £).

(19) **Canalside:** Retail centre with numerous places to eat (Breakfast Club, Gotto, Shane's on Canalside, etc.) and relax alongside the Lee Navigation (various hours, £).

(1) **The Bow Bells:** Classic London pub, serving stone-baked pizzas, homemade burgers and grills (Mon-Thu, noon-11pm, Fri-Sat 11am-11.30pm, Sun noon-10.30pm, £).

Bow Quarter

Bow Quarter

Here East

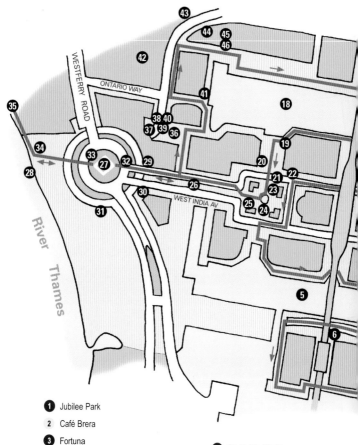

1 Jubilee Park

2 Café Brera

3 Fortuna

4 Torsion II

5 Middle Dock

6 Helisphere

7 South Dock

8 Centauro

9 Sacrificial Anode

10 Churchill Place Shopping Mall

11 Canada Square

12 Canada Square Park

13 The Big Blue

14 Bronze Lions

15 Six Public Clocks

16 Unity of Opposites: Vortex

17 Crossrail Station

18 North Dock

19 Sculptural Railings

20 Two Men on a Bench

21 Returning to Embrace

22 Iberica La Terraza

23 Couple on Seat

24 Draped Seated Woman

25 It Takes Two

26 Man With Arms Open

27 Westferry Circus

28 Canary Wharf Pier

Places of Interest   Food & Drink

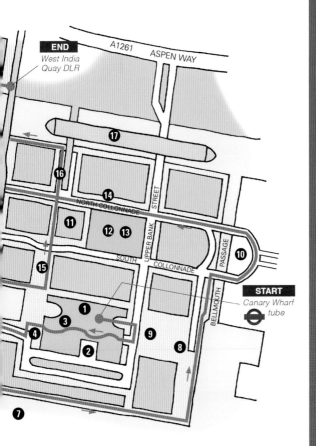

Canary Wharf

CANARY WHARF

Distance: 3 miles (5 km)
Terrain: easy
Duration: 2 hours
Start: Canary Wharf tube (Jubilee)
End: West India Quay DLR
Postcode: E14 5NY

Canary Wharf is located on the site of the former West India Docks, on the Isle of Dogs in East London. There were three separate docks here – the Import (North Dock), Export (Middle Dock) and South Dock – which from 1802 to 1939 comprised one of the busiest dockyards in the world. Its decline began in the '60s, leading to closure in 1980. Redevelopment of the docks into a high-rise business district began in the late '80s, and Canary Wharf – the name comes from the sea trade bringing fruit to the UK from the Canary Islands – is now the city's second financial district and a popular residential area.

From the outset, the 97-acre (39ha) private estate was designed to provide a high quality environment for those who work, live and visit the area, not least by preserving many of the former docks (or parts thereof) as water features. The vision of the developers was to allocate over a third of the area to open spaces, squares and courtyards, embellished with works of art, many of which feature in this walk. Canary Wharf's permanent art collection is one of the UK's largest assemblages of public art and the best place in London to see contemporary sculpture. For lovers of modern art it makes a welcome change from London's copious collection of historic and figurative statuary commemorating long-forgotten royals, politicians and soldiers (et al).

Our walk commences at Jubilee Park and wends its way around the docks and waterways, between skyscrapers and through shopping centres, crammed with cafés, restaurants and bars. It culminates in a visit to the fascinating Museum of London Docklands, before terminating at West India Quay DLR station.

NOTE

Some paths may be temporarily closed due to on-going building works.

Start Walking...

On arrival at Canary Wharf tube station (Jubilee Line), follow the signs to the Upper Bank Street exit – opposite Montgomery Square – from where you go west through **Jubilee Park** ❶ (see box). A short way along, the path passes the entrance to Jubilee Place Shopping Mall, where the popular **Café Brera** 2 on the mezzanine level is a good place for a caffeine fix. A little further along on the right is Helaine Blumenfeld's 2016 sculpture, **Fortuna** ❸, a monumental bronze inspired by the Roman goddess of luck which, according to the artist, 'evokes the fullness and complexity of the human condition'. Exit the park at the western end where you emerge onto Jubilee Plaza. Just to the south of the main tube station exit is Charles Hadcock's **Torsion II** ❹, unveiled in 2011, which has been described as being like a stairway to the stars.

From the sculpture, walk west along Heron Quays Road, opposite **Middle Dock** ❺, towards Heron Quays DLR station. In 1982 Brymon Airways' Captain Harry Gee landed a De Havilland Canada Dash aircraft on Heron Quay to demonstrate the feasibility of the STOLport project, the forerunner to

Jubilee Park

A roof garden built on top of a tube station, Jubilee Park provides a tranquil place for workers and visitors to relax, and also hosts outdoor exhibitions and events. Designed by Belgian architects Jacques and Peter Wirtz, its main feature is a sinuous raised water channel with fountains, contained by stone walls and surrounded by grassy knolls on which to catch the sun. Planting includes ornamental grasses and dogwood, along with around 250 semi-mature trees, including swamp cypress, spring-flowering cherry, evergreen oaks and over 200 dawn redwood trees – an unusual choice in a city park.

London City Airport. A plaque celebrating this achievement can be seen beneath the departure screen in the DLR station. Outside the station is Charles Hadcock's 2009 cast iron artwork **Helisphere** ❻, which combines the characteristics of a sphere with that of a helix – a curve in three-dimensional space. Walking around the

Helisphere

Canary Wharf skyline

sculpture provides a multiplicity of gently changing shapes.

A little way past the station go left down the narrow passage – to the west is the Heron Quays West development, completed in 2019 – which leads to the **South Dock** ❼. Originally an 8-acre (3¼ha) pair of quays separating the South and Export docks of the West India Docks complex, Heron Quays has been extended by a further 3 acres (1¼ ha) to connect with Canary Wharf at its eastern end. Follow the path along the top of South Dock, past Obicà (Italian restaurant) and the East Wintergarden (events venue), and around to the left at the end to Montgomery Square. Here there are a number of sculptures, including Igor Mitoraj's 1984 bronze **Centauro** ❽, which shows the great mythological beast partially incomplete but ready for battle. To the east of the square near Montgomery Street is **Sacrificial Anode** ❾ – an anode (electrode) is attached to a metal object, such as a boat or underground tank, in order to inhibit its corrosion – a beautiful tactile abstract work by Irish sculptor Eilís O'Connell, made largely of stainless steel and bronze.

Sacrificial Anode

Just past the square ascend to Churchill Place over the dock and follow the road around in a semi-circle to North Colonnade past **Churchill**

Canada Square

Originally called Docklands Square, the name was later changed to Winston Square before finally being renamed Canada Square; the developers, Olympia and York, were Canadian. Three of the UK's tallest buildings are located here, the largest of which is One Canada Square, aka Canary Wharf Tower (shown above). At 770ft (235m) it was the tallest building in Britain when completed in 1991 and it remains one of Europe's tallest buildings, although it's since been surpassed by The Shard (Southwark). The distinctive stainless steel pyramid roof of the building is 131ft (40m) high and 98ft (30m) square at the base. There are a number of sculptures in the lobby of One Canada Square.

Place Shopping Mall ❿. Around 150m after you cross back over the dock you come to **Canada Square** ⓫ (see box) and **Canada Square Park** ⓬ where you can see Ron Arad's **The Big Blue** ⓭ sculpture. Installed in 2000, it's a huge asymmetric glass-fibre work resting on a ring of structural glazing which appears to float above the ground, designed both as a skylight for the shopping mall below and as a sculpture above ground. The park is home to an ice rink during the winter months (see icerinkcanarywharf.co.uk). Opposite the park to the north are two magnificent **Bronze Lions** ⓮ outside the HSBC building dating from 2002, replicas of the originals by WW Wagstaff which were cast in 1935 for the bank's Hong Kong HQ.

Continue along North Colonnade and turn left along the eastern edge of Cabot Square to Cubitt Steps and Mackenzie Walk, which swings left past the popular Henry Addington pub. Follow the path east along Middle Dock for around 200m to Reuters Plaza, named after Paul Julius Reuter, founder of the international news agency. Here are Konstantin Grcic's (1999) **Six Public Clocks** 15, based on the iconic Swiss railway clock; each clock has two faces, each showing a different number, although they all show the same (correct) time! From Reuters Plaza head north, past One Canada Square, to Adam's Place, to see Michael Lyons' 2001 work, **Unity of Opposites: Vortex** 16, made from patinated copper. Echoing the writings of Chinese philosophers, it has been described as 'embodying the tensions within modern society between materialistic cravings and spiritual needs'.

From Adam's Place – at the end of which is the new **Crossrail Station** 17 (see box) – turn left (west) on Fisherman's Walk, which runs along the **North Dock** 18. Opposite the North Dock Footbridge on the left of Wren Landing are Bruce McLean's Art Nouveau-like **Sculptural Railings** 19; the 131ft (40m) long charcoal steel railings are heavily worked with shapes, faces, circles and squares in typical McLean style. Also on Wren Landing is Giles Penny's monumental bronze sculpture, **Two Men on a Bench**

20, a large work in the classical figurative tradition, which has a contemplative air but also has an element of fun.

Continue south to Cabot Square – named after the 15th-century Italian navigator and explorer John Cabot (ca. 1450-1500) – which includes a splendid fountain and several works of art. In the forecourt of number 10 is Jon Buck's bronze **Returning to Embrace** 21, which appears to depict a couple locked

---

Crossrail Station

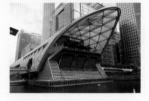

One of the latest additions to Canary Wharf's architecture is the imposing new Canary Wharf Crossrail/Elizabeth Line station in Crossrail Place in the northeast corner of Canary Wharf, alongside the North Dock. The development also acts as a bridge between the Canary Wharf Estate and Poplar to the north (home to nearby Billingsgate fish market). The 1,017ft (310m) long timber lattice roof shelters a striking roof-top garden, which lets in light and rain for natural irrigation, while translucent air-filled pillows allow direct views into and out of the building. When completed the station will be home to a new £1 million permanent public artwork, part of a series of artworks to be displayed at Elizabeth Line stations, dubbed the Culture Line. When the Elizabeth Line is fully operational in autumn 2020 it will connect Canary Wharf to the City of London, the West End, Heathrow and beyond. A restricted service is expected to operate from autumn 2019, terminating at Paddington in the west and Abbey Wood in the east.

Two Men on a Bench

together gazing into each other's eyes, although closer examination reveals a strange fusion of forms, their bodies so far intertwined as to become a single organism. If you're feeling peckish, next door at number 12 is **Iberica La Terraza** 22 , a contemporary Spanish bar-restaurant.

Cabot Square

In the north of the square is Lynn Chadwick's 1984 bronze, **Couple on Seat** 23 , which is sited opposite Henry Moore's bronze, **Draped Seated Woman** 24 , aka 'Old Flo', in the south of the square. The latter work – created in 1957-8 and originally installed on the Stifford Estate in Stepney, East London – was returned to London in 2017 after a 20-year loan to the Yorkshire Sculpture Park. In the southwest corner of the square is Bob Allen's 2002 bronze, **It Takes Two** 25 , a cast taken from the fallen bough of an ancient English Yew listed in the *Domesday Book*. Allen's aim is to reveal the hidden quality

Westferry Circus

Canary Wharf Pier

The pier is served by two commuter services operated by Thames Clipper from central London and Woolwich. Since 2013 boats have run as far as Fulham and Putney (the RB6 service), taking roughly one hour. There's also a service (using smaller boats) from Canary Wharf to Nelson Dock Pier (close to the Doubletree Docklands Hotel) in Rotherhithe, which is opposite Canary Wharf Pier. See thamesclippers. com for information about services.

in wood – here it was the female form that emerged first, later complemented by a male form.

From Cabot Square go west along West India Avenue, where around halfway along (on the central island) is Giles Penny's 1995 bronze, **Man with Arms Open** 26 , a roughly hewn bronze figure with his head thrown back and arms outstretched. A little further along you come to **Westferry Circus** 27 , the western gateway to Canary Wharf for those arriving by ferry at **Canary Wharf Pier** 28 (see box). On the right, outside the inner garden, is Robert Worley's 2009 aluminium work, **Avatar** 29 , portraying a hawk-like beast which has a human form embedded in its back. Opposite, on the south side of West India Avenue, is **Chimney** 30 by Andrew Burton (2008), made from recycled fired bricks and steel. It resembles the brick kilns seen worldwide but is also a tribute to India's tallest brick minaret, the Qutub Minar in

Delhi. To the south of the Circus is Jay Battle's 1999 work, **Vanishing Point** ㉛; made from Derbyshire stone and steel, it looks a little like the shell of a mythical sea creature washed up from the Thames that's been polished to reveal its natural lined core.

In the central garden of the Circus are two more sculptures: Hugh Chapman's elegant bronze, **Growth Form 2012** ㉜ , cast at the nearby Bronze Age foundry in Limehouse; and Do König Vassilakis' 2007 artwork, **Sasso Cosmico** ㉝

Growth Form 2012

(Italian for 'Cosmic Stone'), a bronze and steel 'egg' designed to mirror the surrounding planting, foliage, architecture, sky and clouds. Leaving the Circus opposite the ferry pier you see Ron Arad's soaring **Windwand** ㉞, a 164ft (50m) high needle made of red carbon fibre and installed in 2000. Designed to flex gently in the wind, it subverts one's expectations of what tall objects in this area should do. Just to the north on the riverside are Constance de Jong's two audio benches,

Centurione I

Speaking of the River ㉟. De Jong created a gentle, evocative soundscape using recorded interviews and stories relating to the human experience of these locations, told by people for whom the river is a daily presence.

Retrace your steps across Westferry Circus to West India Avenue and after around 100m go left to **Columbus Courtyard** ㊱. At the western end of the courtyard is Igor Mitoraj's monumental 1987 bronze, **Centurione I** ㊲, portraying a head as an incomplete mask. To the right are two elegant sculptures on loan from Oliver Barratt, **Opening Lines** ㊳ (2010) and **Turning Point** ㊴ (2014). Also in the courtyard is Wendy Ramshaw's steel and perspex work **Columbus Screen** ㊵ from 2000, based on the navigational charts used by the great explorer; it's an apposite choice given the docks' history and their proximity to Greenwich

Hibbert Gate

and its maritime connections.

Leave the courtyard in the northeast corner and go left along the western end of North Dock, where just ahead is Leo Stevenson's bronze and stone **Hibbert Gate** ㊶. It's named after George Hibbert (1757-1837), an alderman of London and a leading promoter of the West India Dock scheme, and was commissioned in 2000 to commemorate the original 1803 entrance to the West India Docks. The bronze ship on top of the arch is the West Indiaman, *Hibbert*, which plied its trade between London and the West Indies from

1785 to 1813, bringing back sugar, rum, cotton, coffee and tropical hardwoods. From the Gate turn left to Hertsmere Road, where you go right and right again on North Dock Walk opposite the **Cannon Workshops** 42 (now a business centre). A little further north (on the left) is the handsome old **Port of London Authority Building** 43.

Ledger Building

Continue along the cobbled walk opposite the Workshops, where the first building on the left is the **Ledger Building** 44, in the northwest corner of the former Import Dock, which takes its name from the building's original use which was to house the ledgers of the West India Docks. This grand building is now home to one of JD Wetherspoon's finest taverns.

Just past the Ledger is the **Museum of London Docklands** 45 (free entry, see box opposite), which tells the fascinating story of the docks that helped make London one of the world's wealthiest cities. It's well worth a visit if you have an hour or two to spare. In front of the museum, opposite the North

Sir Robert Milligan

Food & Drink

2 **Café Brera:** All-day café and bar in Jubilee Place Shopping Mall – handy for a morning latte or a glass of wine at the end of the day (Mon-Fri 6am-8/9pm, Sat 9am-7pm, Sun 10am-6pm, £).

22 **Iberica La Terraza:** Classic and modern Spanish tapas, with a tempting deli counter for takeaways (Mon-Sat 11.30am-11pm, Sun noon-4pm, £-££).

44 **The Ledger Building:** A spectacular pub next door to the Museum of London Docklands, offering JD Wetherspoon's fine ales and pub grub (9am-midnight, 11pm Sun, £).

Dock (home to some old ships), is Richard Westmacott's (1813) bronze of **Sir Robert Milligan** 46 (1745-1809), a leading figure behind the construction of the West India Docks. Installed in 1813, it's a rare traditional statue among the modern art of Canary Wharf. Opposite the statue is St Peter's barge, a Dutch freight barge that has been converted into a floating church (stpetersbarge.org).

From the museum, continue east along the top of the dock – the venue

for a KERB street food market (Tue-Fri
11.30am-2pm) – to West India Quay
DLR station and the end of the walk.
If you prefer to return to Canary Wharf
tube station where you arrived, it's just a
10-minute walk east along the North Dock
and right on Upper Bank Street

Museum of London Docklands

Appropriately housed in a Georgian
'low' sugar warehouse built in 1802
and now Grade I listed, the museum
covers the period from the first port
of London in Roman times to the
closure of the docks in the '80s, and
the area's subsequent redevelopment.
It shows how the Thames became an
international gateway, bringing invaders,
merchants and immigrants to one of
the world's longest-serving ports. See
museumoflondon.org.uk/museum-
london-docklands for information.

Museum of London Docklands

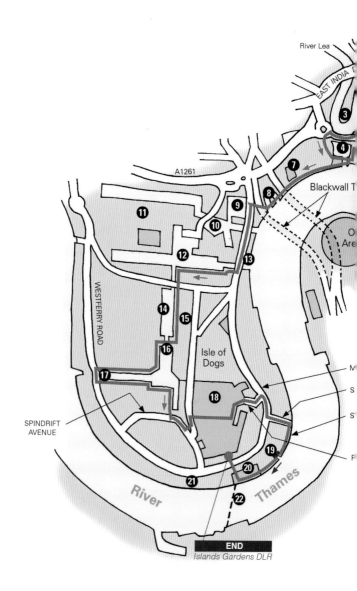

River Lea

EAST INDIA D

A1261

Blackwall T

WESTFERRY ROAD

SPINDRIFT
AVENUE

Isle of
Dogs

O
Are

M

S

S

F

River

Thames

END
Islands Gardens DLR

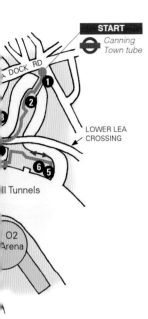

WALK 5

Places of Interest   Food & Drink

Canning Town to Isle of Dogs

CANNING TOWN TO ISLE OF DOGS

Distance: 6 miles (10 km)

Terrain: easy

Duration: 3 hours

Start: Canning Town tube

End: Island Gardens DLR

Postcode: E16 1ED

On this walk we explore some of East London's fascinating former docklands, from Canning Town in the London Borough of Newham to the southern tip of the Isle of Dogs (now part of Tower Hamlets). Prior to the 19th century, Canning Town – named after George Canning (1770-1827), briefly Prime Minister in 1827 or, possibly, his son Charles John Canning (1812-1862), the first Viceroy of India – was largely marshland and accessible only by boat or a toll bridge. The area wasn't developed until the early 19th century, which accelerated with the opening of the Royal Victoria Dock in 1855. Despite being a neighbour of affluent Canary Wharf and the Royal Docks' developments, Canning Town remains one of the most deprived areas in the UK, although it's now undergoing widespread regeneration.

The Isle of Dogs, referred to locally as 'the island', is a geographic area comprising Millwall, Cubitt Town, Canary Wharf and parts of Blackwall, Limehouse and Poplar; it's bounded on three sides by one of the largest meanders in the River Thames, with its southernmost point facing Greenwich. Despite its name, the Isle of Dogs – the first known written mention is in 1520, and it's said that a number of monarchs, including Henry VIII, kept kennels here for their hunting dogs – isn't an island but an 800-acre (324ha) tongue of land. Its industrial development began with the construction of the West India Docks, which opened in 1802, followed by the East India Docks in 1806 and the Millwall Docks in 1868. The docks closed progressively during the '70s, with the last dock ceasing to operate in 1980, after which the area became largely derelict. It was regenerated in the late '80s and '90s, led by the vast Canary Wharf development (see Walk 4).

Starting from Canning Town on Bow Creek, we visit the Leamouth Peninsula and East India Dock Basin before making a detour to Trinity Buoy Wharf, home of the Trinity House workshop from 1803 to 1988. From here we follow the Thames south to Blackwall, past Canary Wharf to Cubitt Town and Millwall. After skirting the Millwall Docks, we enjoy an unexpected rural interlude in Mudchute Park before ending the walk at Island Gardens.

Start Walking...

From Canning Town tube/DLR station – there's a **Costa Coffee**  **1** here if you need a boost – exit onto the path by the River Lea (here called Bow Creek – see box) and cross the river via the red footbridge to the **Leamouth Peninsula** **2** . This is one of two isolated peninsulas – the other is the Limmo Peninsula to the west – formed by the meanderings of Bow Creek. Follow the path along the west side of the Peninsula around to the bottom of the river's loop. Opposite on the Limmo Peninsula is the **Bow Creek Ecological Park** **3** , a former industrial site and now a wildlife haven that attracts flocks of wading birds at low tide, when large areas of mud are exposed.

The path ends beneath the railway bridge that cuts across the Limmo Peninsula. Cross over the Lower Lea Crossing just before the roundabout and take the path around the **East India Dock Basin** **4** – the entrance is near a bus shelter on Blackwall Way. The East India Dock Company was founded in 1803 to trade with the Far East and handled large East Indiamen vessels of up to 1,000 tons. This was the first of the London docks to close (in 1967) and today only the entrance basin remains – it's now a wildlife haven. Continue to the Thames – you'll have a grand view of the O2 Arena from here – and turn left onto the Thames Path (NE Extension) and head east to make a short detour to **Trinity Buoy Wharf** **5** (see box on page 48) located alongside where the River Lea/Bow Creek empties into the Thames. If

River Lea & Bow Creek

The River Lea rises in Leagrave, near Luton, in the Chiltern Hills and follows a path southeast, east and then south through East London. It meets the River Thames at Leamouth, where the final looping section is known as Bow Creek, a 2¼-mile (3½km) tidal estuary that's part of the Bow Back Rivers (see **Walk 3**), a complex of waterways between Bow and Stratford that connect the River Lea to the Thames. The river is one of the oldest navigations in the country, but the creek is tidal and provides insufficient depth for boats at low tide.

you fancy a drink or snack, the wharf's **Fat Boy's Diner** 6 is an authentic American diner.

Retrace your steps to the East India Dock Basin and continue southwest along the Thames Path, where after a few hundred metres you come to **Blackwall Yard** **7** in the historic riverside district of

Isle of Dogs

New Providence Wharf

Blackwall. Blackwall Yard was engaged in shipbuilding (and later repairs) from 1617 to 1987, and Blackwall had a proud maritime tradition; both Raleigh and Nelson are said to have had homes here, while the first colonists of Virginia sailed from Blackwall in 1606. A little further along the path you cross over Blackwall Tunnel South – opened in 1967, it's the newer of a pair of road tunnels underneath the Thames – and pass **New Providence Wharf** ❽ , a riverside residential development consisting of a vast cliff-like, crescent-shaped block and a number of towers.

Just past the wharf take the path inland to Fairmont Avenue and go straight across the roundabout to Yabsley Street. Head west – the route passes over the old Blackwall Tunnel (Northbound), constructed in 1897 – to Preston's Road, where opposite is **Poplar Dock Marina** ❾ . The marina opened in 1997 and connects with the Thames via the **Blackwall Basin** ❿ , a mooring site for barges. Just to the west of the basin are the gleaming towers of **Canary Wharf** ⓫ , which features in **Walk 4** of this book.

From Yabsley Street go left (south) on Preston's Road, where after 150m you cross over the entrance to the Blackwall Basin and, further along, the entrance to **South Dock** ⓬ ; part of the West India Docks, it closed to commercial traffic in 1980 (after which the Canary Wharf development was built on the site). South Dock regularly plays host to medium-sized military vessels visiting London, as it's the furthest point upstream that they can be turned around. Just before the entrance to the South Dock on Coldharbour is **The Gun** 13 . This celebrated gastropub is housed in a striking (Grade II listed) 18th-century building overlooking the Thames, and is allegedly where Horatio Nelson

Trinity Buoy Wharf

The Corporation of Trinity House was established in the 16th century (its charter was granted in 1514 by Henry VIII) to maintain beacons, marks and signs of the sea 'for the better navigation of the coasts of England.' From 1803 to 1988 the corporation's Thameside workshop was located here, making and deploying navigation buoys and seamarks, testing maritime lighting equipment and training lighthouse keepers. The wharf is now a thriving centre for the arts and creative industries, some operating from colourful converted shipping containers ('Container City').

The Gun

enjoyed assignations with Lady Emma Hamilton in an upstairs room. It's a good spot for lunch (booking recommended).

Just south of South Dock is the district known as Cubitt Town, named after William Cubitt (1791-1863), Lord Mayor of London 1860-1862, who was responsible for the development of the area in the 1840s and 1850s. After crossing over the entrance to South Dock, follow the Thames Quay path on the right that runs along the southern edge of South Dock. The path turns left at Millwall Cutting, and from here you cross Marsh Wall (past South Quay DLR station on the right) and walk south along the eastern edge of Millwall Inner Dock. The name comes from the windmills that once lined the western tidal embankment – which, with the Outer Dock, comprised **Millwall Dock** ⓮ (see box), now enclosed by waterfront

Arena Tower

apartment blocks (dubbed 'Canary Wharf's bedroom'), restaurants and shops. Around halfway down you pass the landmark **Arena Tower** ⓯, formerly known as Baltimore Tower, a circular apartment block, and the Lotus Chinese Floating Restaurant. Turn right on Pepper Street past the Manjal Indian restaurant, cross the dock

> ### Millwall Dock
>
> Constructed by John Aird & Co and designed by Sir John Fowler, Millwall Dock opened in 1868. The L-shaped dock has an Outer Dock running east-west and an Inner Dock running north from the eastern end. It originally covered 36 acres (14ha) with a 200-acre (81ha) estate, and the western end of the Outer Dock was connected to the Thames at Millwall by an 80ft (24m) wide channel. Isambard Kingdom Brunel's iron sailing ship *SS Great Eastern* was built here and launched in 1858 (the launch ramp still exists to the south). The dock closed in 1980 after years of decline and today it's a commercial business district, housing small to medium-sized technology, publishing, legal and financial services companies. The dock itself was used as location for boat stunts in the 1999 James Bond film *The World Is Not Enough* and is now home to the Docklands Sailing and Watersports Centre.

via **Glengall Bridge** ⓰ – a Dutch-style double-leaf bascule bridge – and go left past the Pepper Saint Ontiod pub (Ontiod is an acronym for 'On The Isle Of Dogs', while Pepper is from Pepper Street).

Continue along the path which skirts the northern edge of the Millwall Outer Dock. At the western end of the dock is the **Docklands Sailing and Watersports Centre** ⓱ and opposite (across the

Millwall Dock

The Ferry House

Food & Drink

1 Costa Coffee: Outlet of the ubiquitous chain next to Canning Town tube station (5.30am-7.30pm, Sun 6.30am-6.30pm, £).

6 Fat Boy's Diner: Classic '40s-style chrome and neon American diner, offering burgers, hot dogs and milkshakes (Mon-Fri 8.30am-4pm/9pm Thu-Fri, Sat 9am-9pm, Sun 10am-4pm, £).

13 The Gun: Popular riverside gastropub opposite Canary Wharf (020-7519 0075, 11.30am-midnight, Sun closes 11pm, £-££).

21 The Ferry House: The oldest pub on the Isle of Dogs dating back to 1722 – an atmospheric spot for a pint to end the walk (noon-11pm/midnight, £).

Park & Farm **18** (free, daily 9am-5pm, see box opposite). As well as providing a realistic image of a working farm, Mudchute includes a wide range of wildlife habitats, from wetlands and woodlands to open meadows and field margins, while a nearby equestrian centre has around 25 horses and ponies and provides riding lessons. There's also a café.

Follow the path northeast across the park, exit on Pier Street and walk to the end to turn right on Manchester Road. Go left on Seyssel Street and continue on to Storers Quay to return to the Thames Path you followed earlier. Turn right and follow the path south, around the inlet of **Newcastle Draw Dock 19** opposite The Great Eastern pub, and on to **Island Gardens 20**. The 2.8 acre (1.1ha) gardens opened in 1895 and provide spectacular views across the river of the classical buildings of the former Greenwich Hospital, the National Maritime Museum and the Cutty Sark, with Greenwich Park forming a verdant backdrop. The park marks the end of the walk – Island Gardens DLR is just 200m away along Douglas Path.

If you fancy a drink before heading home, **The Ferry House 21**, around 200m west on Ferry Street is recommended. If you have the time, an interesting way to end the walk is to cross

Thames) are Rotherhithe and Surrey Quays. Walk back along the southern edge of the dock and down to the bottom of the finger-shaped inlet to Spindrift Avenue, where you go left and left again, just south of Mudchute DLR station. Cross over the pedestrian crossing on East Ferry Road and enter **Mudchute**

Mudchute Park and Farm

A slice of country life in the former Docklands, Mudchute Park and Farm is London's largest city farm (32 acres/13ha) and one of the largest in Europe, with over 200 animals and fowl. Its inelegant name comes from the fact that it was the dumping ground for Thames mud during the excavation of Millwall Dock in the 1860s, creating an area of fertile, hilly land. The farm – owned by the Mudchute Association, a registered charity formed in 1977 – has an impressive range of animals, including a collection of British rare breeds. (For information see mudchute.org.)

the river via the **Greenwich Foot Tunnel** ㉒ – the entrance (a glass-domed, red-brick rotunda), is next to Island Gardens – to Greenwich. From Greenwich you can return to central London via the Cutty Sark or Greenwich DLR, Greenwich rail or ferry from Greenwich Pier.

Island Gardens

Docklands Sailing and Watersports Centre

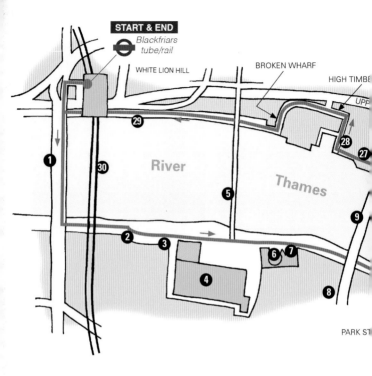

1. Blackfriars Bridge
2. Founder's Arms
3. Bankside Gallery
4. Tate Modern
5. Millennium Bridge
6. Shakespeare's Globe Theatre
7. The Swan
8. Rose Playhouse
9. Southwark Bridge
10. Anchor Bankside
11. Clink Prison Museum
12. Ruins of Winchester Palace
13. Old Thameside Inn
14. Golden Hinde
15. Southwark Cathedral
16. Borough Market
17. The Shard
18. The Old Operating Theatre Museum & Herb Garret
19. London Grind
20. London Bridge
21. Fishmongers' Company
22. Hanseatic Walk
23. The Oyster Shed
24. The Banker
25. Walbrook Wharf
26. Fruiterers' Passage
27. Vintners' Hall
28. Queenhithe Mosaic
29. Blackfriars Pier
30. Blackfriars Thameslink Station

● Places of Interest   ● Food & Drink

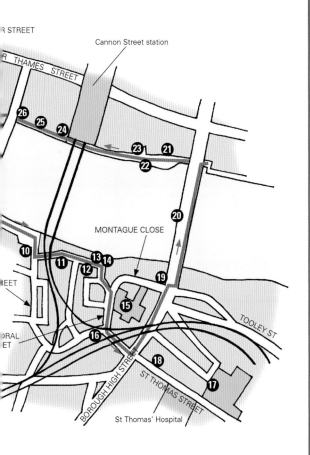

R STREET

R THAMES STREET

Cannon Street station

26 **25** **24**

23 **21**

22

20

MONTAGUE CLOSE

10

11 **13** **14**

12

19

REET

15

DRAL
ET

16

TOOLEY ST

18

ST THOMAS STREET

17

BOROUGH HIGH STREET

St Thomas' Hospital

City & Bankside

Distance: 2¼ miles (3½ km)
Terrain: easy
Duration: 1-2 hours
Start/End: Blackfriars tube/rail
Postcode: EC4V 4DD

CITY & BANKSIDE

This walk follows a section of the River Thames, starting (and ending) at Blackfriars, a historic riverside area named for a 13th-century Dominican priory once located here; the friars wore black habits, hence the name. We cross Blackfriars Bridge to explore Bankside in the borough of Southwark. Bankside – the name was first recorded in 1554 – is one of the oldest settlements in Britain, dating back over 6,000 years. In the Middle Ages it attracted huge crowds to its brothels, animal-baiting pits and playhouses, all of which were banned in the City north of the river. Today, regenerated, pedestrian-friendly Bankside is one of London's most vibrant districts, with a wealth of cafés, restaurants, pubs and visitor attractions.

We stop at magnificent Southwark Cathedral, and then return to the City over London Bridge, where the Romans founded Londinium almost 2,000 years ago. Although the north bank has fewer surviving historic buildings than the south, it's still a fascinating place to visit, with a number of historic livery company halls and one of London's oldest docks.

Although the shortest walk in this book, this is also one of the most compelling. Every time you turn a corner another cultural highlight is revealed, from Tate Modern, Shakespeare's Globe and the Clink Prison Museum, to the *Golden Hinde*, Borough Market and Queenhithe.

Blackfriars Bridge

Start Walking...

Leave Blackfriars station via the Blackfriars Bridge exit on New Bridge Street and cross over colourful **Blackfriars Bridge** ❶, constructed by the distinguished builder Thomas Cubitt and opened in 1869. The bridge achieved notoriety in 1982 when the body of Roberto Calvi, chairman of Italy's largest private bank (Banco Ambrosiano) was found hanging from one of its arches. Courts decided that Calvi – dubbed 'God's banker' due to his close association with the Vatican – had been murdered, although no one has ever been convicted.

On the south side of the bridge take the steps on the left down to the Thames Path (Queen's Walk) and head east, where a short way along is **The Founder's Arms** ❷ , a glass-fronted Young's pub with a large, heated patio. Opposite the pub is **Bankside Gallery** ❸ (free entry, 11am-6pm, entrance in Hopton Street) which offers a changing programme of exhibitions, including contemporary watercolours and original prints. Just past the gallery is the imposing **Tate Modern** ❹ (see box, free), the world's leading contemporary art gallery and one of London's must-see attractions.

Just past the Tate is the **Millennium Bridge** ❺, a spectacular pedestrian steel suspension footbridge linking Bankside with the City of London; opened

Tate Modern

Tate Modern (free entry) opened in 2000 to provide a dedicated space to display the Tate's burgeoning collection of 20th-century art, from Matisse and Picasso to Warhol and Damien Hirst. It has a unique location in the former Bankside Power Station with its iconic 325ft (99m) central tower; the station was designed by Sir Giles Gilbert Scott and generated electricity for London between 1891 and 1981. Today, Tate Modern is the most-visited modern art gallery in the world, attracting over 5.5 million visitors a year, three times as many as Tate Britain upriver at Millbank. See tate.org.uk/visit/tate-modern for information.

in 2000, it offers a perfectly framed view of St Paul's Cathedral's south façade. At the entrance to the bridge is the Tate Community Garden, and beyond it three handsome 18th-century houses. Between numbers 49 and 51 is Cardinal Cap Alley, which used to lead to a brothel called The Cardinal's Cap, so-named because it was owned by Henry Cardinal Beaufort, the Bishop of Winchester. Number 49 has a plaque recording that Sir Christopher Wren lived there while St Paul's Cathedral

Millennium Bridge

was being built, although this is thought to be untrue.

Clink Prison Museum

One of England's oldest prisons, The Clink was the Bishop of Winchester's infamous jail, in use from 1144 to 1780 when it was burnt down in anti-Catholic riots. The name is thought to come from the sound of striking metal, either the prison's metal doors as they closed or the rattle of the prisoners' chains, hence the expression being 'in the clink'. The museum tells the history of the prison, policing, punishment and Southwark's gruesome past. Exhibits include fearful instruments of torture – the museum is a big hit with children! See clink.co.uk for information.

Next door is **Shakespeare's Globe Theatre** 6 which opened in 1997. It's a modern reconstruction and is located around 750ft (230m) from the site of the original theatre; its design is faithful to the 1599 original and is the only building in London permitted to have a thatched roof. Tours are available (see shakespearesglobe.com for prices and info), and if you're ready for lunch, the **Swan** 7 Bar and Restaurant, adjacent to the Globe, is a good choice. Turn right along New Globe Walk and left into Park Street to discover another revived theatre: at number 56 is the site of **Rose Playhouse** 8, Bankside's first Tudor theatre, built in 1587 by Shakespeare's contemporary Philip Henslowe. It was discovered in 1989 and excavated, and now provides a unique venue for theatrical performances.

Leave the Rose Playhouse, turn right and return to Bankside via cobbled Bear Gardens, once the site of a bear-baiting arena (banned in 1835). Turn right and a bit further along you pass under **Southwark Bridge** 9, opened in 1921. Around 100m past the bridge the path turns inland on Bank End where, on the right, is the **Anchor Bankside** 10, sole survivor of the numerous riverside inns that existed here in Shakespeare's time – there has been a tavern here for over 800 years. Almost opposite the pub go under the railway viaduct to Clink Street and the **Clink Prison Museum** 11 (entry fee, 10am-6pm, 9pm weekends, see box).

Past the museum the street is flanked by Victorian warehouses and, on the right, the **Ruins of Winchester Palace** 12 – former London residence of the Bishop of Winchester – gaze down majestically over the street, an unexpected rare fragment of history dating back to 1109. A little further along on Pickfords Wharf is Nicholson's **Old Thameside Inn** 13, another characterful pub; facing it in St Mary Overie dock is the **Golden Hinde** 14 (entrance fee, 10am-6pm), a replica of the galleon in which Sir Francis Drake circumnavigated the globe between 1577 and 1580. Drake (1540-1596) is most famous as second-in-command of the English fleet that destroyed the Spanish

Globe Theatre

Southwark Cathedral

Southwark Cathedral

One of the city's most historic churches, Southwark Cathedral is the mother church of the Anglican diocese of Southwark and has been a place of worship for over 1,000 years, although surprisingly it's only been a cathedral since 1905. It had its first official mention in the *Domesday Book* of 1086 as the 'minster' of Southwark, although the current building is mainly Gothic, dating from 1220 to 1420. There's an abundance of memorials in and around the cathedral, and a popular café at the rear. For more information see cathedral. southwark.anglican.org.

Armada in 1588, but he was also a notable privateer, authorised by Elizabeth I to attack and loot ships belonging to England's enemies – in effect the Spanish. Heading away from the river, Cathedral Street leads to **Southwark Cathedral** ⑮ (see box), which is strategically sited at the oldest crossing point of the Thames.

Go straight ahead and as Cathedral Street merges into Bedale Street, on the right you'll see the main entrance to **Borough Market** ⑯ , first recorded in 1276, although a market is believed to have existed here since the 11th century. It's a must-visit for those who care about the quality and provenance of their food, and contains a wealth of restaurants, cafés, taverns and fast food outlets – an excellent place for a snack or lunch.

At the end of Bedale Street turn left on Borough High Street, from where you get a fine view of **The Shard** ⑰ just a few hundred metres away – at 1,017ft (310m) it's Britain's tallest building. Cross to St Thomas Street, heading towards The Shard, and around 50m along on the left is **The Old Operating**

Theatre Museum & Herb Garret ⑱ , housed in the attic of the early 18th-century church of the old St Thomas' Hospital. The atmospheric museum offers a unique insight into the history of medicine and surgery (entrance fee, see oldoperatingtheatre.com for opening times). Return to Borough High Street and turn right towards the river; you pass the **London Grind** ⑲ café-bar-restaurant on the left, just before **London Bridge** ⑳ (see box on page 58).

Walk across the bridge to the north side and descend the spiral staircase on the right to the Thames Path, where you go west (under the bridge) past the imposing **Fishmongers' Company** ㉑ livery hall (1834). This section of the path

Borough Market

London Bridge

The Romans built the first 'permanent' wooden bridge across the Thames here in around 55AD, which has been followed by a succession of later bridges. The first stone bridge was commissioned by Henry II and opened in 1209 during the reign of King John, having taken 33 years to complete. The bridge had a chapel in the middle dedicated to Thomas à Becket (St Thomas), which became the official starting point for pilgrimages to Becket's shrine at Canterbury Cathedral. The 'old' London Bridge stood for over 600 years before being replaced in 1831 by a stone-arched bridge, which in turn was supplanted by the current box girder bridge, designed by Lord Holford and built in 1973.

HANSEATIC WALK EC4

CITY OF LONDON

Thames Path

is named the **Hanseatic Walk** 22 after the Hanseatic League (1358-1669) – a commercial and defensive confederation of merchant guilds and market towns in north-western and central Europe – whose self-governing London enclave, the Steelyard, was located nearby. After a short distance you pass **The Oyster Shed** 23 , a good pit stop for a late lunch.

Walbrook Wharf

Turn right into All Hallows Lane and go left along Steelyard Passage under Cannon Street Station, where you emerge by **The Banker** 24 , a popular Fuller's pub.

Follow the riverside path signposted **Walbrook Wharf** 25 , leading to Three Cranes Walk, which takes you along a covered walkway through the City of London's rubbish depot; the walkway is closed periodically when refuse is being loaded onto barges, when barriers come down and warning lights flash (an alternative route is shown on a sign). A bit further along you come to Southwark Bridge, where you turn right to follow the path under the road (just before the stairs) along brightly-lit **Fruiterers' Passage** 26 – named after the Worshipful Company of Fruiterers, it's lined with ornate tiles and decorative panels showing historic images of the bridge and this part of the City. At the end of the passage go left and follow the path along Three Barrels Walk under the grand neo-classical portico of **Vintners' Hall** 27 , home of the Worshipful Company of Vintners, to cobbled

Queenhithe Mosaic

Food & Drink

2 **The Founder's Arms:** Enjoy a panoramic view across the Thames to St Paul's as you tuck into a delicious brunch (9am-11pm/midnight, £).

16 **Borough Market**: There are plenty of lunch choices at the foodies' favourite market (Mon-Fri 10am-5/6pm, Sat 8am-5pm, closed Sun, £-££).

19 **London Grind:** Cult riverside espresso bar, cocktail bar and restaurant, housed in an imposing former bank (Mon-Thu 7am-midnight, Fri 7am-1am, Sat 8am-1am, Sun 9am-7pm, £).

23 **The Oyster Shed**: Bright riverside bar with stripped floors, offering seafood and classic British dishes (Mon-Fri 9am-11pm, Sat 10am-5pm, Sun 11am-8pm, £-££).

From Queenhithe go left along High Timber Street and left again down Broken Wharf, where you join Paul's Walk alongside the Thames. Follow the path under the northern end of the **Millennium Bridge** **5** and a few hundred metres further along you come to the new **Blackfriars Pier** **29**, served by river bus services (Mon-Fri). Just past the pier the **Blackfriars Thameslink Station** **30** (opened in 2012) spans the river, beyond which the four pairs of red columns in the river are the remains of the old London, Chatham and Dover railway bridge of 1864. A few steps further along is **Blackfriars Bridge** **1**, where you go up the stairs to the bridge and right to Blackfriars Station, where the walk ends.

Blackfriars Station

Queenhithe. This was once a thriving dock with a history going back to Saxon (or possibly even Roman) times; it remained in use into the 20th century and is the only surviving inlet on the modern waterfront. The 100ft (30m) long **Queenhithe Mosaic** **28** illustrates the key events and personalities who built, used and lived around the dock.

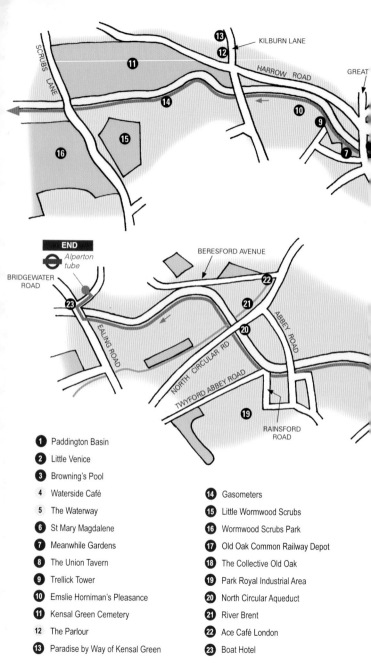

1 Paddington Basin
2 Little Venice
3 Browning's Pool
4 Waterside Café
5 The Waterway
6 St Mary Magdalene
7 Meanwhile Gardens
8 The Union Tavern
9 Trellick Tower
10 Emslie Horniman's Pleasance
11 Kensal Green Cemetery
12 The Parlour
13 Paradise by Way of Kensal Green

14 Gasometers
15 Little Wormwood Scrubs
16 Wormwood Scrubs Park
17 Old Oak Common Railway Depot
18 The Collective Old Oak
19 Park Royal Industrial Area
20 North Circular Aqueduct
21 River Brent
22 Ace Café London
23 Boat Hotel

● Places of Interest   ○ Food & Drink

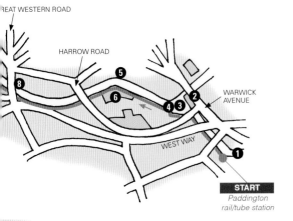

GREAT WESTERN ROAD

HARROW ROAD

5

8

6

4 **3** **2**

WARWICK
AVENUE

WEST WAY

1

START
Paddington
rail/tube station

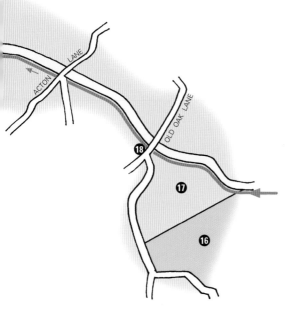

ACTON LANE

OLD OAK LANE

18

17

16

Grand Union Canal

WALK 7

Distance: 6 miles (10 km)
Terrain: easy
Duration: 3 hours
Start: Paddington rail/tube
End: Alperton tube
Postcode: W2 1HQ

GRAND UNION CANAL

The Grand Union Canal is Britain's longest at 137 miles (220km), linking London with Birmingham, passing through rolling countryside, industrial towns and peaceful villages – and some 166 locks. The canal wasn't constructed as a single entity but is the result of the amalgamation of several independent waterways (built at the end of the 18th and early 19th centuries) which took place between 1894 and 1929. The term 'Grand Union' now generally refers to the canal from the River Thames at Brentford to the junction with the Digbeth Branch in Birmingham. The canal has several arms – or branches – of which the Paddington Arm is one, slicing through west London and providing a green corridor for both people and wildlife.

The Paddington Arm is 13½ miles (22km) long, running from Hayes to Little Venice – where it joins the Regent's Canal – and the Paddington Basin. Like all Britain's canals, the Grand Union failed to survive the competition from the railways and road transport in the 20th century. However, since the '60s it has been revitalised by an army of volunteers and today is alive with pleasure boats, walkers, cyclists and joggers.

Our walk begins at Paddington Station and follows the canal west via Maida Vale, Westbourne Park and Ladbroke Grove, bordering magnificent Kensal Green Cemetery and Wormwood Scrubs Park. From Kensal Green we follow the canal as it skirts the Old Oak Common Railway Depot at Harlesden and the vast Park Royal Industrial Area, to Alperton, where it passes over the North Circular Aqueduct and the River Brent, before concluding at Alperton tube station.

Grand Union Canal

Start Walking...

Leave Paddington Station by the exit for **Paddington Basin** ❶, the terminus of the Paddington arm of the Grand Union Canal, and now a hotspot for commercial and residential development. Turn left to walk alongside the basin, under a few road bridges, until you reach **Little Venice** ❷ (see box) and **Browning's Pool** ❸. The pool (and the island in the middle) – named in honour of the poet Robert Browning, who lived nearby – links the Grand Union Canal and the Regent's Canal, which runs east for 8.6 miles (13.8km) to join the Thames at Limehouse (see **Walks 9 & 10**).

Waterside Café

One of London's most exclusive residential areas, Little Venice is an unexpected haven of calm and beauty. The canal is lined with weeping willows and flanked by graceful, stuccoed Regency mansions, many designed by noted architect John Nash. Houseboats

Little Venice

A tranquil throwback to a time when London was a collection of villages, the name Little Venice is used rather loosely, but technically speaking it's where the Regent's Canal meets the Grand Union Canal and the Paddington Basin. Nowadays it's used in a wider context to describe an area of less than a square mile in Maida Vale, although the name didn't come into general use until after the Second World War.

painted in bright red, dark green and navy blue dot the canal, some with window boxes bursting with flowers, others adorned with elaborate nameplates, while ducks, geese and swans drift languidly by. Continue straight ahead along the southern edge of Browning's Pool, where near the western end is the **Waterside Café** ❹ – a handy place for a morning coffee but don't expect anything fancy.

From the café continue west under Westbourne Terrace Road and along the Grand Union Canal towpath – the paved path runs along the southern side of the canal (which is lined with narrowboats on both sides), parallel with Delamere Terrace. Just past Lord Hills Road there's a footbridge over the canal leading to **The Waterway** ❺, a popular gastropub with a splendid terrace and tasty brunch. Continue along the towpath

Little Venice

past the red and white spire of **St Mary Magdalene** ⑥ church, designed by George Edmund Street and completed in 1873. For the next few hundred metres the path is bordered by grassland and trees, before going under Harrow Road and the Westway (A40) flyover. Just after the Great Western Road the towpath runs alongside **Meanwhile Gardens** ⑦, a community garden featuring a wildlife garden with pond and a popular skate bowl. There are steps up to the Great Western Road bridge, where **The Union Tavern** ⑧ – a Fuller's pub with a lovely waterside terrace – is on the opposite side.

Continue west along the edge of Meanwhile Gardens and after around 200m you get a good view of **Trellick Tower** ⑨, a 322ft (98m) tall tower block regarded as a local landmark (or eyesore). Grade II* listed, it

Trellick Tower

was designed by Ernő Goldfinger in true concrete Brutalist style and opened in 1972 providing 31 floors of predominantly social housing. Apart from a few pubs there's not much in the way of facilities along the towpath, although you could make a detour

Westbourne Park

Emslie Horniman's Pleasance

The word 'pleasance' derives from French and means 'secluded garden' or 'enclosed plantation', and this one is named after Emslie John Horniman MP (1863-1932) who created it in 1911. Extending to an acre (0.4ha), it contains a handsome walled Arts and Crafts style garden, Grade II listed, designed by architect Charles Voysey (1857-1941).

just past Trellick Tower to Golborne Road, where there's plenty of cafés and restaurants. Continue along the canal, where some 200m past the end of the gardens there's a footbridge over the canal to Harrow Road. Opposite the footbridge on the south side, take a detour along Wedlake Street and turn right onto Kensal Road to visit **Emslie Horniman's Pleasance** ⑩ (7.30am-dusk, see box), a delightful little urban park that's the starting point for the annual Notting Hill Carnival.

Return to the towpath and after another 400m, pass under Ladbroke Grove where on the north bank is the vast **Kensal Green Cemetery** ⑪ (see box opposite), one of London's Magnificent Seven cemeteries created in the 1830s and 1840s to alleviate overcrowding in church graveyards. One of the capital's most distinguished garden cemeteries, Kensal Green opened in 1833, making it London's oldest public burial ground. At 77 acres (31ha), it's also the largest and the most opulent, containing around 250,000 graves. If you have a spare hour or two, it's well worth a visit (the entrance is in Harrow Road off Ladbroke Grove).

Paradise by Way of Kensal Green

If you're ready for lunch, the **Parlour** 12 on Regent Street is recommended. It's a short walk north along Kilburn Lane. On the corner of Regent Street is the celebrated **Paradise by Way of Kensal Green** 13, a charming, bohemian gastropub. With a rabbit warren of intimate spaces decorated in eclectic, shabby-chic style, Paradise – its name is a nod to G K Chesterton's poem *The Rolling English Road* – attracts the beautiful people of Kensal Green but, unfortunately, is only open for lunch from Friday to Sunday.

Back on the canal, the towpath winds past a Sainsbury's superstore and, some 300m further on, two disused **Gasometers** 14. These icons of yesteryear – beloved by some, loathed by others – date back to 1845 when the Kensington Gas Works opened (they now await their fate). A few hundred metres further on – and some distance south over the railway tracks – is **Little Wormwood Scrubs** 15 (21 acres/8.8ha, 7.30am-dusk), former common land that was once part of Wormwood Scrubs Park before it

Kensal Green Cemetery

Inspired by the Père Lachaise Cemetery in Paris, Kensal Green Cemetery was designed by John Griffith. Its grounds were the work of Richard Forrest, head gardener at Syon Park, and were laid out as an informal park with a number of formal features and a profusion of specimen trees. Today, vast tracts have been set aside as nature reserves, hence its apparent unkempt appearance. You can still see the landing piers by the canal bank where coffins were delivered by barge. The cemetery contains a huge number of buildings, tombs, memorials and mausoleums – many Grade II or II* listed – where many prominent members of 19th-century society were laid to rest. (For more information and opening times, see kensalgreencemetery.com.)

Kensal Green Cemetery

was cut adrift by the construction of the West London Railway in 1844. Opposite, on the north side of the canal, is St Mary's Roman Catholic cemetery (est. 1858) just to the west of Kensal Green Cemetery.

At Scrubs Lane the towpath goes under a road bridge and railway bridge and continues alongside the railway tracks. On the other side of the railway lines is **Wormwood Scrubs Park** 16

Old Oak Common Railway Depot

(unrestricted, see box), and beyond it HM Prison Wormwood Scrubs, open since 1874. Here the canal is lined by a series of industrial units although there's a small nature reserve alongside the **Old Oak Common Railway Depot** 17 and rail sidings. A bit further along, the path runs under Old Oak Lane, where just past the bridge is **The Collective Old Oak** 18, a vibrant community of 500 with shared living spaces. As the canal heads northwest out of London it continues through a largely industrial landscape, although still lined with trees, passing under Acton Lane in Harlesden. Part of the London borough of Brent, Harlesden has a lively cosmopolitan population and a vibrant Caribbean culture (it's London's unofficial reggae music capital).

From here, the canal cuts through the **Park Royal Industrial Area** 19, the largest business park in London occupying 1,200 acres (500ha) with over 1,700 businesses. Park Royal has been home to some household names, such as McVitie's and Guinness, although the vast Guinness Brewery, designed by Giles Gilbert Scott, opened in 1936 and closed in 2015. After Park Royal you arrive at the busy North Circular Road (A406) where the **North Circular Aqueduct** 20 – which the IRA attempted to blow up in 1939 – carries the canal over the traffic-clogged road. Just past the North Circular, a concrete footbridge crosses over the confluence with the **River Brent** 21 (see box opposite) and from the towpath there's a fine view of Wembley Stadium to the north. Around 500m northeast along the North Circular Road is the world-famous **Ace Café London** 22, established in 1938 and a popular hangout for rockers, bikers, petrol heads and rock 'n' roll fans ever since.

Ace Café

The final section of canal through Alperton is another soulless stretch lined by vast warehouses and industrial buildings, with very few residential moorings. After passing a number of blocks of flats you come to the Ealing Road bridge, where you take the steps up to Ealing Road, go right over the canal

---

Wormwood Scrubs Park

At around 200 acres (80ha), Wormwood Scrubs is the largest open space in the borough of Hammersmith and Fulham, and one of the largest areas of common land in west London. Known locally as the Scrubs, it's been a public open space since 1879. The name derives from the 15th-century Wormholtwode, meaning 'a snake-infested wood', and while the snakes have long gone, the Scrubs does have the status of a Local Nature Reserve and is home to an important population of common lizards, some 20 varieties of butterfly, and over 100 resident and visiting bird species. The common offers a wide range of sporting facilities – soccer, cricket and rugby pitches, and a pony centre for disabled riders – plus the Linford Christie Stadium athletics centre.

Food & Drink

4 **Waterside Café:** Housed on a narrowboat at Little Venice, this is all about the view and the location (9am-6pm, £).

5 **The Waterway:** Noted for its superb weekend brunch served 10am-1pm (Mon-Fri 10.30am-11pm, Sat 10am-11pm, Sun 10am-10.30pm, £-££).

12 **The Parlour:** Just off Kensal Rise, offering an all-day menu of contemporary British food and craft ales (Tue-Sun 10am-10pm, closed Mon, £).

River Brent

A tributary of the Thames, the Brent (see **Walk 12**) – the name is Old English meaning 'sacred waters' – is one of London's longest rivers, flowing 18 miles (29km) through west and northwest London, rising at the junction of Dollis and Mutton Brooks in Hendon and flowing in a generally south-westerly direction to join the Tideway stretch of the Thames at Brentford. The Brent links with the main line of the Grand Union Canal at the end of Green Lane in Hanwell on its way to Brentford.

Alperton roughly marks the halfway point of the Paddington Arm of the Grand Union Canal, which continues for another 7 miles (11km) through urban and suburban west London to Bull's Bridge in Hayes.

Alperton

and follow the road around to the right opposite the **Boat Hotel** **23** – last chance saloon on this walk (although not highly recommended). Alperton tube station and the end of the walk is around 100m up on the left.

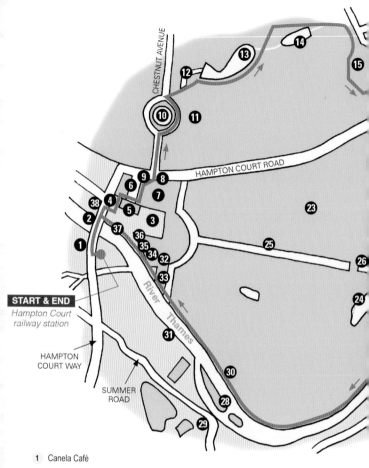

1. Canela Café
2. Hampton Court Bridge
3. Hampton Court Palace
4. Ticket Office
5. Rose Garden
6. Tiltyard
7. The Wilderness
8. Lion Gate
9. Maze
10. Diana Fountain

Places of Interest   Food & Drink

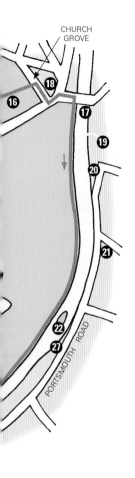

CHURCH GROVE

11 Bushy Park
12 Diana Car Park
13 Heron Pond
14 Leg of Mutton Pond
15 Hampton Wick Royal Cricket Club
16 The King's Field
17 Kingston Bridge
18 White Hart Hotel
19 Hogsmill River
20 Kingston Town End Pier
21 St Raphael's
22 Ravens Ait Island
23 Hampton Court Park
24 The Rick Pond
25 Long Water
26 Golden Jubilee Fountain
27 Harts Boatyard
28 Thames Ditton Island
29 Ye Olde Swan
30 Pavilion
31 The Albany
32 Privy Garden
33 Tijou Screen
34 The Pond Gardens
35 Little Banqueting House
36 Great Vine
37 Turks Pier
38 The Mute Swan

WALK 8

Hampton Court & Bushy Park

Distance: 5½ miles (9 km)
Terrain: easy
Duration: 3 hours
Start/End: Hampton Court rail
Postcode: KT8 9AE

HAMPTON COURT & BUSHY PARK

ampton – the name is thought to come from the Anglo-Saxon words *hamm* (a large bend in a river) and *ton* (a farmstead or settlement) – has been settled for over 4,000 years, although the village of Hampton dates from the Middle Ages. Modern Hampton has evolved to include three villages – Hampton, Hampton Wick to the east and Hampton Hill to the north – collectively known as the Hamptons. At their heart is Bushy Park, London's second-largest royal park after Richmond Park, and Hampton Court Palace, Britain's finest surviving Tudor building.

Our walk commences at Hampton Court station just south of the River Thames, from where we head north over Hampton Court Bridge through Hampton Court Palace gardens to Bushy Park; the route then goes north, around the Diana Fountain, and along the Heron and Leg of Mutton Ponds. From the ponds we walk south to Hampton Wick and join the riverside Barge Walk near Kingston Bridge to return to Hampton Court along the Thames. The Barge Walk borders Hampton Court Park – home to the Long Water – passing a number of islands in the river and the palace gardens, before arriving back at Hampton Court station.

Hampton Court Palace & Gardens

Start Walking…

From Hampton Court railway station, turn right on Hampton Court Way. If you fancy coffee or breakfast, the **Canela Café** **1** opposite the station is recommended. Cross the River Thames via **Hampton Court Bridge** **2** – the fourth bridge on this site – designed by Sir Edwin Lutyens and engineer W. P. Robinson and opened in 1933. The entrance to **Hampton Court Palace** **3** (see box) is around 50m along on your right through the gates, where the **Ticket Office** **4** is on the left. Ticket prices are high and you need at least a couple of hours to see the main attractions and can easily spend a whole day exploring the palace and gardens.

Hampton Court Palace

Hampton Court Palace (Grade I listed) is a vast royal palace covering 6 acres (2.5ha) besides the Thames. Built in 1514 for Cardinal Thomas Wolsey – Lord Chancellor and favourite of Henry VIII – it was seized by the king in 1529 when Wolsey fell from favour. Henry made it his main London residence and greatly enlarged it. William III made extensive changes in the following century (he intended Hampton Court to rival Versailles) but lost interest in 1694 after the death of his wife Mary II, leaving the palace in two distinct contrasting architectural styles: domestic Tudor and Baroque. The palace was opened to the public in 1838. For more information see hrp.org.uk/hampton-court-palace.

Rose Garden

Continue past the ticket office to the lovely **Rose Garden** **5** and, beyond it, the **Tiltyard** **6** and **The Wilderness** **7**, and exit the gardens via the **Lion Gate** **8**, just to the right of the **Maze** **9** (fee), to Hampton Court Road. From the Lion Gate, cross over the road to Chestnut Avenue (designed by Sir Christopher Wren) and walk up to the pond, where the **Diana Fountain** **10** sits in the centre. The glorious fountain was designed by Hubert Le Sueur in 1637 for Charles I and features a bronze statue of the goddess Diana, surrounded by bronzes of four boys, water nymphs and shells. The fountain and pond are located in the southern section of **Bushy Park** **11** (see box on page 72).

Take the right-hand road around the pond and head right to the **Diana Car Park** **12**, which has a kiosk where you can get a coffee (summer 8.30am-6pm, winter 8.30am-4pm). Rather than walk through the car park, take the narrow path almost opposite the kiosk and go left at the end on the main path that runs along the southern edge of **Heron Pond** **13**, frequented by swans, herons, coots and other waterfowl. You can obtain a fishing permit that includes Heron Pond, Long Water, Rick Pond and the Leg of Mutton Pond (the season runs from 16th June to

Heron Pond

14th March), although the first section of Heron Pond is designated a 'boating pool' where fishing is prohibited. The pond is one of an early group of hydro-engineered ponds in Bushy Park and neighbouring Hampton Court Park, including the Long Water, fed by water from the distant River

Bushy Park

A traditional deer park extending to 1,100 acres (445ha), the name Bushy Park was first recorded in 1604, although its origins date from 1491 when Giles d'Aubrey (Lord Chamberlain to Henry VII) enclosed 400 acres (162ha) of farmland. When Henry VIII appropriated Hampton Court Palace from Cardinal Wolsey in 1529, he also assumed ownership of the three parks that surrounded it: Hare Warren, Middle Park and Bushy Park, which make up today's Bushy Park. Henry created a deer chase and built a wall around the park, a section of which remains. Today, the park strikes a balance between wilderness and decorum, its rough grassland and plantations complemented by formal avenues of lime and chestnut trees. For more information see royalparks.org.uk/parks/bushy-park.

Colne via the man-made Longford River (see box opposite).

Continue along the pond to the end where the path crosses over a channel connecting Heron Pond to the **Leg of Mutton Pond** 14. To the south and north of the ponds you may see groups of red and fallow deer, part of a herd of around 300, descended from those in Henry VIII's time. Follow the path along the top of the pond and after around 200m cross back over the water channel along Cobbler's Walk. Just before Sandy Lane, take the right-hand fork south to **Hampton Wick Royal Cricket Club** 15 and follow the path around the eastern edge of the playing field. At the bottom of the field take the narrow track to the left and walk along the top of **The King's Field** 16 to Church Grove, where you turn right to reach Hampton Court Road. At the end, cross the road, turn left and walk up to the roundabout, then turn right onto Horse Fair which leads over **Kingston Bridge** 17 (see box on page 74). If you fancy lunch, the **White Hart Hotel** 18 on the opposite side of the roundabout is worth a small detour.

White Hart Hotel

Just before the bridge, go right on Barge Walk which runs south along the Thames through a grove of trees, and provides a good view of Kingston on the opposite side of the river. After some 200m, the **Hogsmill River** 19 empties into the river from the opposite bank; at 6 miles (10km) in length, it's a tributary

Food & Drink

1. **Canela Café**: Inexpensive café serving tasty breakfasts and a range of Latin-American fusion dishes (Tue-Sun 8.30am-5.30pm, closed Mon, £).

18. **White Hart Hotel:** Handsome Fuller's establishment in Hampton Wick offering British favourites and modern European cuisine (Mon-Fri 7am-11pm, Sat-Sun 8am-11pm, £).

38. **The Mute Swan:** Historic pub opposite Hampton Court Palace serving good food and ales (Mon-Thu 11am-11pm, Fri-Sat 11am-midnight, Sun 11am-10.30pm £).

Longford River

Longford River is an artificial waterway that diverts water 12 miles (19km) from the River Colne at Longford near Colnbrook to Bushy Park and Hampton Court Palace. Designed by Nicholas Lane, the waterway was constructed for Charles I in 1638-39 as a water supply for Hampton Court; the Long Water was created in the 1660s and the water features in Bushy Park in 1710.

of the Thames rising in Ewell. Soon after you pass **Kingston Town End Pier** 20, the HQ of Turk Launches Ltd., which operate cruise boats along the Thames, and the flamboyant Italianate tower of **St Raphael's** 21, a Catholic church designed by Charles Parker. Soon after passing the church you come to **Ravens Ait Island** 22, a 2-acre (0.8h) wedding and corporate events venue.

Over to the right in **Hampton Court Park** 23 (see box on page 74) is **The**

Rick Pond 24, a popular fishing and model yacht racing venue; it lies just south of the glorious **Long Water** 25 canal, at the eastern end of which is the **Golden Jubilee Fountain** 26 which was unveiled in 2002 to celebrate Queen Elizabeth II's 50 years on the throne. Back on Barge Walk, just past the island (on the opposite bank) is the Thames Sailing Club and **Harts Boatyard** 27, a contemporary pub and restaurant, where the Thames is lined with pleasure boats and working barges. Opposite Harts Boatyard the path splits: take the left-hand fork to continue along the river where the narrow Thames Path is lined with trees, shrubs and wild flowers.

A few hundred metres further along there's a high fence on the right that shields exclusive Hampton Court Palace Golf Club from the hoi polloi, while opposite is Thames Ditton Marina. Just before the marina is the delightfully-named Seething Wells, where the Lambeth Waterworks Company built filter beds in the 1850s to purify river water before piping it to London. The path here

Thames Ditton Island

loops round to the north, passing **Thames Ditton Island** 28 (see box opposite), a residential ait (river island) where the chalet homes are raised to protect them against flooding. The island is connected to the opposite river bank by a handsome 1939 suspension bridge next to the 13th-century **Ye Olde Swan** 29 pub.

Kingston Bridge

There has been a bridge over the Thames at Kingston since at least the 12th century (and probably earlier) and until Putney Bridge was opened in 1729 this was the only crossing of the Thames between London Bridge and Staines Bridge (14 miles/22½km upriver). It was a wooden bridge until the 1820s when it was replaced by the current Portland stone bridge (Grade II* listed), designed by Edward Lapidge and opened in 1828.

To the right of the path opposite the island is Pavilion Terrace, where the red-brick **Pavilion** 30 is the sole survivor of four garden pavilions built by Christopher

Wren for William III in the last few years before the king's death in 1702. Just past the island is the Dittons Skiff & Punting Club (founded 1923) and other boathouses, and **The Albany** 31, a popular riverside gastropub. Around 300m further on you arrive back at Hampton Court Palace, where there's a good view of the palace, although high walls conceal the **Privy Garden** 32 from view. From Henry VIII's day until the 18th century, only the monarch and his or her closest advisors and confidantes

Hampton Court Park

Also known as Home Park, Hampton Court Park (750 acres/303ha) consists mainly of grassland scattered with large oak trees and has remained virtually unchanged since opening to the public in 1894. An outstanding feature of the park is its great avenues of some 550 lime trees (planted in the 1660s by Charles II), which flank the Long Water canal for around 1km.

were allowed entry here. Where the garden meets the Thames it's bounded by magnificent semi-circular wrought iron gates and railings designed by French Huguenot iron-worker Jean Tijou (ca. 1660-1725), known as the **Tijou Screen** 33. It consists of 12 decorative wrought iron panels – its central motifs symbolise parts of the UK – and was installed at the edge of the Privy Garden in 1702.

Just past the Privy Garden are **The Pond Gardens** 34, once a medieval fish farm that supplied fish for Friday 'fast' days on the Christian calendar (in the Middle Ages a non-meat day was considered a fast day). Here you also find

Tijou Screen

the **Little Banqueting House** ㉟ where William III entertained his courtiers, now a private events venue. Next to the Pond Gardens is the **Great Vine** ㊱ – thought to be the oldest and largest grape vine in the world – which was grown from a cutting planted by Capability Brown in 1769 to the point where its trunk is now 12 feet (3.6m) in circumference and its longest branch measures around 110 feet (33½m).

Thames Ditton Island

Thames Ditton Island owes its existence to Henry VIII who straightened and deepened the Thames just downstream from Hampton Court, to allow his barges uninterrupted passage from Westminster to Hampton Court Palace. The two smaller islands are Boyle Farm Island to the south, which has a single house, and tiny Swan Island – home to the old ferryman until 1911 – in the middle.

Near the end of Barge Walk you pass **Turks Pier** ㊲, where you can get a ferry to Kingston or Richmond. Opposite the palace on Hampton Court Way is **The Mute Swan** 38 , a characterful pub with a spacious bar, upstairs restaurant and courtyard terrace. Continue left over **Hampton Court Bridge** ❷ to Hampton Court railway station on the left, from where you began the walk.

River Thames

1 Carreras Cigarette Factory

2 KOKO

3 Statue of Richard Cobden

4 Leyas

5 Blues Kitchen

6 Camden Head

7 Jazz Café

8 Electric Ballroom

9 Elephants Head

10 Poppies

11 Regent's Canal

12 Camden Lock

13 Turnover Bridge

14 Camden Market

15 Dingwalls

Places of Interest   Food & Drink

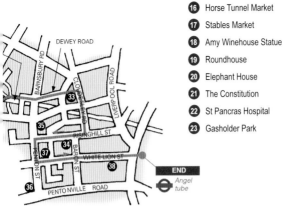

16 Horse Tunnel Market
17 Stables Market
18 Amy Winehouse Statue
19 Roundhouse
20 Elephant House
21 The Constitution
22 St Pancras Hospital
23 Gasholder Park

24 St Pancras Lock
25 Camley Street Natural Park
26 Granary Square
27 The Lighterman
28 Words on the Water
29 King's Place
30 Battlebridge Basin
31 London Canal Museum
32 Islington Canal Tunnel
33 Culpeper Park
34 Chapel Market
35 Liman Restaurant
36 The Lexington
37 Craft Beer Co.
38 Crystal Maze Live Experience
39 Camden Passage Antiques Market

WALK 9

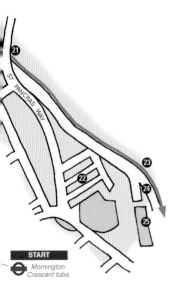

Regent's Canal
(Camden to Islington)

REGENT'S CANAL (CAMDEN TO ISLINGTON)

Distance: 3½ miles (5½ km)
Terrain: easy
Duration: 2 hours
Start: Mornington Crescent tube
End: Angel tube
Postcode: NW1 2JA

This walk commences in Camden Town in northwest London, an area that was once the manor of Kentish Town, acquired through marriage in 1749 by Sir Charles Pratt, 1st Earl Camden (1714-1794), after whom it's named. He developed some fields as a residential district in 1791, which formed the beginnings of the town. The London borough of Camden was created in 1965 from the former metropolitan boroughs of Hampstead, Holborn and St Pancras, which were previously part of the County of London. Until the mid-20th century, Camden Town was an unfashionable district, but began to gain popularity with the opening of Camden Market in 1973. Today, it's one of London's coolest neighbourhoods, with an abundance of trendy cafés, restaurants, pubs and a wealth of music venues, not forgetting the ever-popular market.

In 1816, the Regent's Canal (8½ miles/14km) – named after the Prince Regent (later George IV) – was built through the area, linking the Paddington arm of the Grand Union Canal with the River Thames at Limehouse in East London, which was also important during the early development of the railways. In the 20th century the canal faced increasing competition from rail and road transport and after the Second World War there was a rapid decline in commercial traffic, which by the late '60s had all but ceased. After years of decline and neglect the canal has been resurrected as a peaceful haven for boaters, walkers and cyclists, while the industrial buildings and warehouses that lined the canal have largely been replaced with modern housing or converted into apartments. Meanwhile, the area's industrial base has been replaced by service industries such as retail, tourism and entertainment.

After exploring Camden High Street and the markets, our walk follows the Regent's Canal towpath from Camden via King's Cross to the Angel in Islington. From Islington the canal continues to wend its way east to its final destination in Limehouse, which is covered in Walk 10 (Regent's Canal East). The first section of the canal, from Little Venice to Camden, is included in another of our walks' books, *London's Green Walks*.

Start Walking…

From Mornington Crescent tube station, cross over Hampstead Road and walk down a short way to see the former **Carreras Cigarette Factory** ❶ (see box), one of London's most imposing Art Deco buildings. Retrace your steps to the tube station and head north up Camden High Street, where the first building on the right is **KOKO** ❷, one of the city's best live music venues. It opened in 1900 as a music hall and has done stints as a theatre, cinema and rock venue. Outside the club, near the kerb, is a marble **Statue of Richard Cobden** ❸ (1804-1865), a Radical and Liberal statesman who's

Blues Kitchen

best known for his defence of free trade, illustrated by his fight to repeal the Corn Laws that were abolished in 1846. A little way past the statue on the right is **Leyas** ❹ , a coffee shop that's perfect for a caffeine shot and mid-morning snack.

Continuing along Camden High Street, after around 250m you come to the **Blues Kitchen** ❺ on the left, opposite Pratt Street, a blues bar serving Cajun comfort food. On the corner of Pratt Street is the **Camden Head** ❻, an impressive Victorian (1849) gin palace with high ceilings, a striking red bar top, attractive glasswork, mirrors and tiles, and a large beer garden. This excellent pub is also home to the Camden Comedy Club, featuring top class acts seven days a week. The entertainment comes thick and fast in Camden, where round to the left in Parkway is the **Jazz Café** ❼, an intimate venue for jazz, soul and reggae. Back on Camden High Street, just past Camden Town tube station, is the iconic **Electric Ballroom** ❽, established in the '30s and

---

Carreras Cigarette Factory

The factory is a striking example of early 20th-century Egyptian Revival architecture, inspired by the contemporary fashion for Egyptian-style buildings and decorative arts, built in 1926-28 by the Carreras Tobacco Company. The front of the building was lined with a colonnade of 12 large columns, decorated with papyrus leaves painted in bright colours with Venetian glass decoration. Dominating the entrance to the building were two large (8.5ft/2.6m) bronze statues of cats, stylised versions of the Egyptian god Bastet (or Bast). The factory closed in the early '60s and was converted into offices and stripped of its Egyptian decoration, but in the late '90s it was largely restored to its former Art Deco glory, including replicas of the famous black cat statues. The building isn't open to the public but can be admired from the road.

Electric Ballroom

Walk 9

Camden Lock

Camden Market

Created as an arts and crafts market in the '70s, Camden Market is London's largest and coolest bazaar with over 1,000 outlets; it's a popular destination for trendy young Londoners and visitors, attracting over 100,000 bargain hunters at weekends. It comprises several adjoining markets (Camden Lock Market, Camden Canal Market, Horse Tunnel Market, Stables Market, etc.), collectively called 'Camden Market' or 'Camden Lock', which occupy former warehouses and workshops secreted in a warren of souk-like narrow lanes. People flock here to buy an eclectic jumble of bric-a-brac, antiques and collectables, retro and vintage fashion, ethnic art, rugs and kilims, jewellery, furniture, music and food (especially street food), while Stables Market is the centre of the alternative fashion scene. For more information see camdenmarket.com.

still one of the capital's best-loved venues, hosting club nights and live bands. It looks dated now but remains a cool place with a great 'rock 'n' roll club' atmosphere, super sound system and huge dance floor.

Around 100m further north, on the corner of Hawley Crescent, is the **Elephants Head** ❾, dating from 1832 and once owned by the Camden Town Brewery that made 'Elephant Ale' in the 1800s. It's yet another music pub, where in-house DJs spin classic vinyl nightly. On the opposite side of the crescent is **Poppies** ❿, one of the city's best fish and chip shops. A few minutes past the pub you reach the **Regent's Canal** ⓫.

Just before the canal, go left along the towpath towards **Camden Lock** ⓬ (real name Hampstead Road Locks) – the only remaining working double pair of locks on the Regent's Canal – and cross over the **Turnover Bridge** ⓭. The bridge was created to allow barge horses to cross the canal (and avoid Dingwalls Wharf) while still towing, and was originally the only point on

the canal heading east where the towpath was on the right-hand (or south) side. Over the bridge you enter Camden Lock Market, one of the several markets that make up **Camden Market 14** (see box). On the right is the legendary **Dingwalls** ⓯ in Middle Yard, a historic music venue established in 1973. Nowadays it's more comedy club than music venue, although on the right night with the right band the old magic shines through, reprising the atmospheric powerhouse of yesteryear.

Camden Market

Follow the lanes around to the **Horse Tunnel Market** 🔟, with its striking horse sculptures, and **Stables Market** 🔟, where you can see Scott Eaton's bronze of **Amy Winehouse** 🔟 (1983-2011), unveiled in 2014. The British singer and songwriter – who died tragically in 2011 from alcohol poisoning at the age of just 27 – lived in nearby Camden Square. From the market return to Chalk Farm Road and turn left to see the **Roundhouse** 🔟 (see box), another of London's legendary gig venues

From the Roundhouse retrace your steps to Regent's Canal on the opposite side of the road and turn left just before the bridge. Once past the food stalls, the clamour of trade gives way to blissful calm as you head east along the towpath. Immediately opposite on the south side is the European HQ of the music video station MTV, formerly the TV-am studios. A short way along, you pass the Hawley and Kentish Town locks, two double locks converted into single locks (the second lock is now a weir). Just beyond the lock and adjacent to Kentish Town Road bridge is **Elephant House** 🔟, a two-storey terracotta brewery building dating from 1900 that produced Elephant Ale – there's a superb elephant's head carving over the main portal on Kentish Town Road – and now home to Elephant House Studios. On the opposite bank, just past the bridge,

Roundhouse

Art meets architecture at the Grade II* listed Roundhouse, constructed in 1847 as a Victorian steam-engine repair shed – round because it contained a railway turntable – and revived as an arts venue in the '60s. The Roundhouse was a showcase for many top bands in the '60s and '70s, from rock legends the Rolling Stones and Jimi Hendrix to punk stars such as the Clash and the Ramones, and witnessed some seminal musical moments. Redeveloped in 2006, the Roundhouse features an exciting programme of cabaret, comedy, alternative theatre, dance, circus, installations and new media, and is once more one of the gems of the London gig circuit.

are the futuristic housing pods of Grand Union Walk Housing.

You pass under two more bridges, Camden Street and Camden Road, and soon after, the River Fleet runs (not visible) beneath the canal. A major

Elephant House

tributary of the Thames, it was an open river in the 1600s and was said to be around 25ft (8m) wide in Camden. Continuing along the towpath and under the St Pancras Way bridge you pass the **Constitution ㉑**, a traditional canalside pub with a nice beer garden. From here the towpath heads southeast to St Pancras, a long bleak section lined with nondescript housing, offices and vast warehouses. Originally, it was flanked solely by industrial buildings – nobody wanted to live alongside a canal carrying dirty horse-drawn barges loaded with chemicals, dynamite and coal – but nowadays the proximity to water and relative peace has made it desirable for developers.

St Pancras Hospital

As you approach St Pancras, the ugly brown building on the south bank is a former Royal Mail sorting office, now a warehouse for fashion retailer Ted Baker, beyond which is sprawling **St Pancras Hospital ㉒**, formerly the St Pancras Workhouse, dating from 1777 (some original buildings survive). The area around St Pancras and King's Cross railway stations – built some 30 years after the canal – has been transformed since the late '90s but it isn't until you emerge from the shadows of the St Pancras railway lines that you

Food & Drink

④ **Leyas:** Hip coffee shop noted for its artisan baking (Mon-Fri 7.30am-5.30pm, weekends 9am-5.30pm, £).

⑭ **Camden Market:** The market is home to a wealth of eateries and international street food, particularly the West Yard's Global Kitchen (10am-late, £).

㉖ **Granary Square:** Home to an abundance of bars, cafés and restaurants, plus the ever-popular KERB street food market (various times, £-££).

㉟ **Liman Restaurant:** Serving tasty mezze and grills, the Liman in Islington is highly recommended (Mon-Fri noon-3pm, 5-11pm, Sat-Sun noon-11pm, £).

Gasholder Park

Granary Square

come to a section of the towpath bordering more attractive and imaginative redevelopment.

Just past the railway bridge is **Gasholder Park 23**, which must qualify as one of London's most unique 'parks'. It's housed in Gasholder (gasometer) No. 8, constructed in the 1850s, the frame of which houses the stunning park by day and transforms into a subtly lit events space by night. A nearby trio of gasholders have been transformed into luxury apartments. Opposite the park is an inlet, originally the St Pancras Basin and now a mooring area for narrowboats, which is located just before **St Pancras Lock 24** and the 'Lock Keeper's Cottage' (a former back-pumping station to push water back up the canal). And just past the lock is Somers Town Bridge, a footbridge leading over the canal to **Camley Street Natural Park 25** (see box). (To access the bridge from the towpath you need to retrace your steps to just past the lock and take the left-hand path.)

Just past the park the canal takes a sharp turn to the left, where there's a large stepped terrace (just before a bridge) that leads to **Granary Square 26**, a former canal basin that's now part of the vast King's Cross redevelopment. It's home to a plethora of bars, cafés and restaurants, including Caravan, the Granary Square Brasserie and Dishoom, plus the ever-popular KERB street food market (Wed-Fri, noon-2pm). The square is animated with over 1,000 choreographed fountains, which create a spectacular show at night when they're illuminated. On the right

Camley Street Natural Park

A tranquil green haven in the most urban of locations, the park is situated immediately behind St Pancras International Station and was a coal depot from Victorian times until the '60s. Occupying a narrow strip of land (2 acres/0.8ha), Camley Street is an urban wildlife sanctuary and education centre run by the London Wildlife Trust that opened in 1985. A variety of habitats co-exists here, including wetlands, marshland, a wildflower meadow, woodland, reed beds around a pond and a garden area. The reserve's celebrities include the rare earthstar fungi, bats and around 50 bird species, including reed warblers, kingfishers, geese, mallards and reed buntings.

Battlebridge Basin

near the canal is the **Lighterman** ㉗, a modern gastropub offering an all-day menu, including breakfast, weekend brunch and Sunday roasts. Almost opposite the Lighterman, permanently moored on the canal, is **Words on the Water** ㉘, London's most unusual 'bookshop' housed on a 100-year-old Dutch barge.

Chapel Market

London Canal Museum

Opened in 1992, the absorbing Canal Museum tells the story of the capital's canals from their early days as vital trade routes – long before motorised vehicles, motorways and even railways – through years of decline and abandonment, to their resurrection as corridors of leisure for boaters, walkers and cyclists. Housed in a former Victorian ice warehouse, the museum tells the story of the Regent's Canal and the people who lived and worked on it. See canalmuseum.org.uk for details.

From the square the path continues east, passing under Maiden Lane Bridge (York Way), where the canal regains some of its peaceful aura. Opposite is the celebrated **King's Place** ㉙, an arts and conference venue built on what was previously the Great Northern Distillery Wharf. A little further along is **Battlebridge Basin** ㉚, constructed in 1820 and now a narrowboat mooring. Battlebridge is the old name for the King's Cross area and legend has it that the Iceni queen Boudicca fought the Romans here and lies buried beneath platform number 9

at King's Cross Station. The basin is home to the **London Canal Museum** ㉛ (see box), which is well worth a visit if you have more than a fleeting interest in canals. You can reach it via York Way: head south, turning left on Wharfdale Road and left again on New Wharf Road.

A few hundred metres past the basin, the towpath goes under Caledonian Road and 100m further on the canal disappears into the **Islington Canal Tunnel** ㉜, just before Muriel Street. From here, it runs for some 2,900ft (878m) beneath the Angel area of Islington, before resurfacing just past Duncan Terrace Gardens. Follow the path on the left to Muriel Street, cross over and continue along the footpath which follows (more or less) the route of the canal via Basketball Park to Maygood Street. At the end of the street, cross Barnsbury Road and continue along Dewey Road and enter the green oasis of **Culpeper Park** ㉝, named after the 17th-century botanist Nicholas Culpeper (1616-1654). Exit the park on Cloudesley Road and turn right, crossing Tolpuddle Street to White Conduit Street (through the car park) and on to **Chapel Market** ㉞. A street market (Tue-Sat 9am-6pm, Sun 8.30am-4pm), Chapel Market sells fresh produce, along with inexpensive household goods and clothes. On

Sundays (10am-2pm), Islington Farmers' Market is held at the Penton Street end.

Continue to the western end of Chapel Market, where the **Liman Restaurant** 35 (Mediterranean-Turkish cuisine) is well worth a stop if you're peckish. Go left on Penton Street, heading south to Pentonville Road. On the corner is the superb **Lexington** 36, a classic London boozer specialising in American craft beers and whiskies. Retrace your steps and turn right on White Lion Street, where you pass the **Craft Beer Co** 37, a pub specialising in micro-brewed cask ales, small batch craft beers and over 400 global bottles – a beer lover's mecca – and tasty burgers, too. Continue along the street, where around 50m before the end (on the right) is the **Crystal Maze Live Experience** 38, based on the popular '90s TV show; according to the website, you 'grab some friends, run around like loons, yell like there's no tomorrow, complete a variety of tricksy challenges and end up wearing some sensational satin bomber jackets' – sounds great!

Camden Passage Antiques Market

At the end of the street cross over Islington High Street to Angel tube station, which marks the end of the walk. If it's a Wednesday or a Saturday, you may wish to visit the **Camden Passage Antiques Market** 39, just a short walk north along the high street.

Regent's Canal

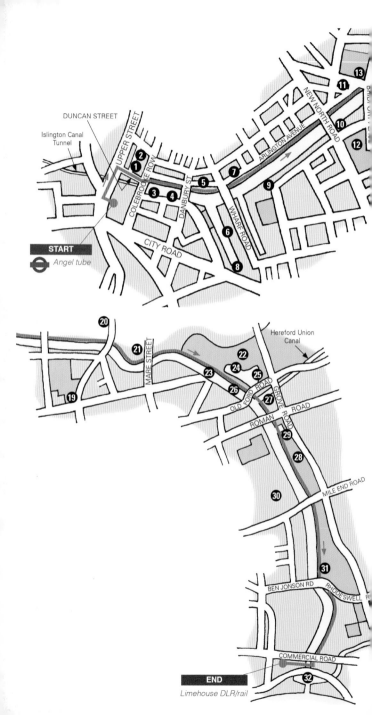

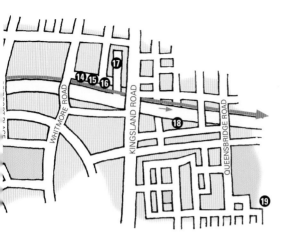

WALK 10

Regent's Canal (Islington to Limehouse)

Distance: 5 miles (8 km)
Terrain: easy
Duration: 3 hours
Start: Angel tube
End: Limehouse DLR/rail
Postcode: N1 9LQ

Angel Wings sculpture, Angel Centr[e]

The Regent's Canal – named after George IV, Prince Regent and the monarch who inspired the Regency era – was a key part of England's canal network. It was built to link the Paddington arm of the Grand Union Canal (at Little Venice) with the Thames at Limehouse, East London – a distance of 8½ miles (14km). The first section from Paddington to Camden opened in 1816 and the final section from Camden to Limehouse in 1820. By the 1840s the railways were already taking traffic from the canals and several attempts were made to turn the canal into a railway during the 19th century. The canals manage to survive despite increasingly stiff competition from the railways and (in the 20th century) road transport, although it was an uphill battle. The last horse-drawn commercial traffic was carried on the canal in 1956, and by the late '60s commercial traffic had all but vanished.

The canal was regenerated in the '70s and '80s as a leisure facility and the towpaths opened to the public. Today, Regent's Canal is one of London's best-kept secrets, a peaceful haven often hidden by the surrounding buildings, beloved by boaters, walkers and cyclists looking to escape the capital's busy streets. The mixture of boat moorings – people still live along the canal in narrowboats – heritage buildings, canalside pubs and cafés, and the connection with nature make for a delightful setting.

This walk follows the eastern section of the canal from the Angel, Islington, where it emerges from the Islington Canal Tunnel, to its final destination in Limehouse. The middle section of the canal from Camden to Islington is covered in Walk 9, while the first section of the canal, from Little Venice to Camden, is included in another of our walking guides, *London's Green Walks*.

Stat Walking...

Exit Angel tube station and turn right along Islington High Street and right again where it leads into Duncan Street. If you fancy a coffee to get fired up, the renowned **CoffeeWorks Project** **1** is a little way further along the high street on the right, opposite the tram shed which dates from 1850 and is now a sofa showroom. A bit further along, the street becomes Camden Passage, the venue for **Camden Passage Antiques Market** **2** (see box).

Camden Passage Antiques Market

Hidden down a cobblestoned backstreet, visiting the Passage is to step back to bygone years. The market is held on Wednesdays (7am-4pm) and Saturdays (6.30am-5pm), when you'll find a multitude of stalls selling an eclectic mix of antiques and collectables – vintage clothes, handbags, jewellery, silver, porcelain, glass and assorted bric-a-brac – alongside a range of elegant Georgian antiques shops, pubs, cafés and restaurants. See camdenpassageislington.co.uk for more information.

Island Queen

Return to Duncan Street and head east to where the road crosses over Duncan Terrace to Colebrook Row; just over the zebra crossing a path leads down to the **Regent's Canal** **3** towpath. The canal resurfaces here after its 2,900ft (878m) subterranean journey from Muriel Street in Barnsbury, beneath the Angel area, via the Islington Canal Tunnel. As you walk towards Danbury Street bridge, past a chain of live-in narrowboats, on the opposite bank you can see the **Plaquemine Lock** **4**, a New Orleans-themed pub named after a lock that opened not here, but on the mighty Mississippi (USA) in 1909.

Take a detour to Danbury Street, turning left onto Noel Road. The playwright Joe Orton (1933-67) – author of *What the Butler Saw* – lived (and died) at number 25: he was murdered here by his lover, Kenneth Halliwell. Retrace your steps along Noel Road, crossing Danbury Street, to the **Island Queen** **5** at number 87, a handsome, traditional Victorian tavern with a nice terrace, offering a wide selection of draught world beers and superior pub grub. Back on the canal, just before the **City Road Basin** **6**, are City Road locks, which mark the halfway point of the canal between Little Venice and Limehouse. The City Road Basin (4 acres/1.6ha) opened in 1820 to serve the City of London, less than a mile away to the southeast (it's now used for canoeing by the Islington Boat Club). A bit further

City Road Basin

Shepherdess Walk Park mosaic

on, just after Wharf Road bridge, is **The Narrowboat** ⑦, the only pub situated directly on the canal in Islington; a freehouse, it serves a range of cask ales and craft beers and good seasonal food. Opposite the pub is the Wenlock Basin, opened in 1826 when the City Road Basin became full; it has private narrowboat moorings at the north end, while at the southern end on Wharf Road is the celebrated **Victoria Miro** ⑧ art gallery.

Continuing along the towpath, you pass a footbridge over the canal which leads to **Shepherdess Walk** ⑨; on the right are some early 19th-century houses and after about 100m, next to number 107, a narrow subway runs underneath the houses and emerges in Shepherdess Walk Park. The park was once a pleasure garden, and in 1842 two public baths – the largest in London for 90 years – were opened here, but it's now best known for its striking mosaics by Tessa Hunkin.

Hitchcock sculpture, Gainsborough Studios

Back on the canal, a few hundred metres further along is Sturts Lock, then the New North Road bridge. Just past the road on the south side of the canal is a huge apartment building, **Gainsborough Studios** ⑩, built on the site of the original film studios which opened in 1924 and were demolished in the '90s. The studios' name is displayed in large metal letters on the roof – visible from Shoreditch Park (see below) – and in the courtyard there's Antony Donaldson's (2003) huge steel bust of film director/producer Alfred Hitchcock (1899-1980), who made many films at the studios. The area to the north of the canal is **De Beauvoir Town** ⑪ (see box), which has a mixture of social housing, old Victorian

De Beauvoir Town

An interesting area – its name comes from Richard Benyon de Beauvoir (1769-1854), MP and landowner – De Beauvoir was developed in the mid-19th century, much of it as a carefully planned new town designed to attract prosperous residents. The development was based around handsome De Beauvoir Square and primarily built in the Jacobethan style; it's now part of a conservation area with many splendid buildings, noted for its many fine pubs, cafés, restaurants and antique shops. One of the district's historical claims to fame is that in May 1907, the Brotherhood Church (Southgate Road – now demolished) hosted the Fifth Congress of the Russian Social Democratic Labour Party, the forerunner of the Communist Party, attended by Lenin, Stalin and Trotsky.

factories and warehouses, and new waterfront developments.

The next exit, onto Baring Street, provides access to **Shoreditch Park** ⓬ (19 acres/7.7ha), south of the canal – created in the '70s, it's one of Hackney's largest parks – and to popular Rosemary Gardens which contain some lovely trees. In the southeast corner of the gardens is the award-winning **Rosemary Branch Theatre & Bar** ⓭, originally a Victorian music hall (1854) where Charlie Chaplin performed.

The next bridge you come to is Whitmore Road and just after, right on the Kingsland Towpath, is the aptly named **Towpath Café** 14 . It's a narrow open-fronted café with tables by and even *on* the canal, courtesy of a floating pontoon. Next door is **The Barge House** 15 , a modern canalside restaurant with more outdoor seating and a reputation for a superb weekend brunch, which is followed by **Arepa & Co** ⓰, a quirky café/bar with hammocks and a terrace offering Venezuelan mains and light bites.

Towpath Café

Next up is the **Kingsland Basin** ⓱, aka the Kingsland Road Basin (dating from 1822), which now provides mooring for residential narrowboats and is home to a number of housing developments. Continue along the towpath under busy Kingsland Road and Haggerston Road, where opposite is the imposing

Bridge Academy, a community school, and Hoxton Docks, behind which is **Haggerston Pool** ⓲ (Grade II listed) in Laburnum Street. A handsome redbrick building opened in 1904 as public baths, it was closed in 2000 and is still awaiting funds for renovation.

Broadway Market

Established on an old drovers' route into the city, Broadway Market has been home to market traders since the 1890s, and provides a unique blend of tastes and cultures. It hosts a cornucopia of independent cafés, restaurants, pubs and independent shops, and is the venue for one of the city's best Saturday markets (9am-5pm). Launched in 2004, it boasts over 100 stalls selling artisan foods, street food and drinks, along with vintage and designer togs, bric-a-brac, books, flowers, and arts and crafts (see broadwaymarket. co.uk).

To the south of the canal, just after Queensbridge Road, is Haggerston Park, home to **Hackney City Farm** ⓳ (Tue-Sun 10am-4.30pm), one of the few places where you can experience farming in the city. Some 500m further on is Acton's Lock just before Cat & Mutton Bridge, where the celebrated **Broadway Market** ⓴ (see box) is just to the north. From the bridge the canal continues southeast, going under a railway bridge before Cambridge Heath Road/Mare Street. Just before the railway bridge are some horse ramps – small recesses with steps going into the canal, a common sight near railway bridges – which facilitated the rescue of barge horses which had fallen into the canal waters after being startled by steam engines.

Viktor Wynd Museum of Curiosities

At number 11 Mare Street, just north of the bridge, is one of the city's most bizarre museums, the **Viktor Wynd Museum of Curiosities** 21 (fee, Wed-Sun noon-10.30pm), with a tiny café, cocktail and tapas bar on the ground floor. The museum is the home of the Last Tuesday Society, founded in 1873 at Harvard University (USA) by William James and brought to London as a pataphysical (the branch of philosophy dealing with an imaginary realm additional to metaphysics) organisation in autumn 2006 by Viktor Wynd and David Piper. The museum focuses on the pre-enlightenment origins of the museum as a Wunderkabinett – a mirror to a world so suffused with miracles and beauty that it defies categorisation (for enlightenment – or further bemusement – see thelasttuesdaysociety.org). Just past Mare Street the canal is lined with new developments, before the urban landscape is transformed and you reach magnificent **Victoria Park** 22 (7am to dusk, see box).

Around halfway along the towpath frontage of Victoria Park you come to the Bonner Gate and bridge (opposite Sewardstone Road), where the Greek replica **Dogs of Alcibiades** 23 statues – presented to the park in 1912 by Lady Regnart – guard the main entrance. The Victoria Park Market (Sun 10am-4pm) is held here, between Bonner and Gore

---

Victoria Park

Known colloquially as 'Vicky Park', Victoria Park in the borough of Tower Hamlets is a beautiful space extending to 218 acres (86ha). Designed by James Pennethorne and opened in 1845, it's the oldest park in Britain created specifically for the public – hence its nickname 'the people's park'. It remains at the heart of East London life and has long been a centre for political meetings and rallies. It once had several 'Speakers' Corners', hosting socialist soapbox stars such as William Morris and Annie Besant, and later became the venue for politically-oriented rock concerts. Now Grade II listed, it's a stunning example of a formal London park, reminiscent of Nash's Regent's Park. Although created as a place for people to breathe clean air, it became a centre for horticultural excellence and boasts some delightful open parkland, wide carriageways, lakes, gardens and ornate bridges over canals. It's also an important leisure hub and hosts a wide range of formal and informal sports, as well as sponsored activities, festivals and concerts throughout the year.

Pavilion Café, Victoria Park

Regent's Canal & Victoria Park

Food & Drink

1. **The CoffeeWorks Project:** Independent coffee house near the Angel (7.30am-6pm, Sat-Sun 9am-6pm £).

14. **Towpath Café:** Situated on the towpath in De Beauvoir Town, this café has a reputation for good coffee and delicious Mediterranean-inspired food (Tue-Sun 9am-5pm – but worth checking – closed Mon and from Nov to March, £).

15. **The Barge House:** Canalside restaurant, next door to the Towpath Café, offering modern British cuisine (Tue, Sun 10am-5/6pm, Wed-Sat 10am-11pm, closed Mon, £).

25. **Pavilion Café:** Located in Victoria Park, the Pavilion serves delicious all-day breakfasts and tasty lunches (8am-4pm, Sat-Sun 8am-6pm, £).

park is also home to the splendid **Pavilion Café** 25 , located in a domed pavilion on the lake near Crown Gate West.

Near the end of the park is the **Old Ford Lock** 26 and some preserved lock keeper's cottages and stables (both Grade II listed). Shortly after Old Ford Road is a footbridge over the **Hertford Union Canal** 27 (1.25mi/2km), opened in 1831, which connects the Regent's Canal with the River Lee Navigation to the east. Just past the channel is **Mile End Park** 28 (see box on page 94), a linear park extending 2½ miles (4km) from Wennington Green in the north to just before Limehouse Cut in the south, bordered by the canal for much of its length.

Queen Mary University London

Gates. In the southwest of the park is the West Boating Lake, which contains an island that's home to a **Chinese Pagoda** 24 , a 2012 replacement for the original which was moved here from Hyde Park in 1847 and demolished in the '50s. The

Heading south along the towpath under the Roman Road bridge, you pass the Ecology Park and lake, and then a traditional East End boozer, **The Palm Tree** 29 ; it isn't noted for its beer or food, but is a real Cockney experience. Just before Mile End Road, over to the right, is the campus of **Queen Mary University London** ③⓪, a constituent college of the University of London with a history dating back to 1785. The focal point of the university is the Queens' Building, aka the People's Palace, constructed in 1886 and badly damaged by fire in 1931. Rebuilt and reopened in 1936, it has a unique Art Deco Great Hall, where everything from orchestral to rock concerts is staged. It also houses the elegant Octagon, originally the QMUL library, inspired by the Reading Room of the British Museum. Marooned within the university grounds, just off Westfield Way, is the Jewish Sephardi Novo Beth Chaim Cemetery, which opened in 1733 after the nearby Velho (Old) Sephardi (1657) cemetery was full.

Mile End Park

This award-winning park is actually a series of parks, built largely on bomb sites from the Second World War. It's divided into sections with different themes such as art, ecology, sport and wildlife, linked by grassy spaces, water features and the spectacular Green Bridge – aka the 'banana bridge' – over busy Mile End Road. The 90-acre (36ha) linear park was planned in the '40s but only began to be created at the end of the millennium, and its on-going development mirrors the regeneration of East London.

Ragged School Museum

Further south, just before Ben Jonson Road is the **Ragged School Museum** ③① (free, Wed-Thu 10am-5pm, first Sun of month 2-5pm, raggedschoolmuseum.org. uk). This little-known museum (opened in 1990) is housed in a group of warehouses that once formed the largest 'ragged' school in London. It was founded by Thomas John Barnardo (1845-1905), an Irish philanthropist who worked as a 'missionary' among the poor of London's East End. He opened his first 'ragged'

school in 1867 – later to become Dr Barnardo's Homes – to provide free basic education to poor children. The museum tells the story of the schools and the broader social history of the East End.

Once past the museum the canal veers south away from Mile End Park and wends its way to Limehouse, which takes its name from lime kilns established here in the 14th century. Just before the canal enters the **Limehouse Basin** ③② – which links the River Lee (via the Limehouse Cut), the Regent's Canal and the River Thames – you pass the Commercial Road Lock, the penultimate lock before the Thames. The basin lies between the Docklands Light Railway – which incorporates one of the oldest railway viaducts in the world designed by Robert Stephenson in the 19th century – and historic Narrow Street to the south, where the Limehouse Basin Lock provides access to the Thames. The basin is now a marina, with mooring for river, canal and sea-going craft.

At the end of Regent's Canal, cross the footbridge and follow the path west along the northern edge of Limehouse Basin to Branch Road and Limehouse DLR station, which marks the end of the walk. If you fancy a drink, Husk Coffee is on the north side of Commercial Road, just before Limehouse DLR. Alternatively, you can head south of the basin where there are some fine pubs on Narrow Street.

Limehouse Basin

START
Hanwell Rail

STATION APPROACH

UXBRIDGE
ROAD

BOSTON ROAD

Grand Union
Canal

M4 MOTORWAY

A4
GREAT WEST RD

LONDON RD

1 Alwyne Road Park

2 Wharncliffe Viaduct

3 The Viaduct

4 Old Lock-keeper's Cottage

5 Hanwell Lock 97

6 The Fox

7 Elthorne Park

8 Osterley Lock 98

9 Boston Manor Playing Fields

10 Boston Manor Park

11 Boston Manor House

12 Brentford Gauging Lock

13 Siracusa

14 Syon Park

15 Brentford Dock

16 Thames Locks, Brentford

● Places of Interest   ● Food & Drink

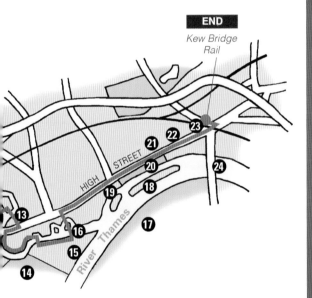

River Brent

WALK 11

Distance: 5 miles (8 km)
Terrain: easy
Duration: 2-3 hours
Start: Hanwell rail
End: Kew Bridge rail
Postcode: W7 3EB

RIVER BRENT

The River Brent runs for 18 miles (29km) through west and northwest London, rising at the junction of Dollis Brook and Mutton Brook in Hendon (Barnet) and flowing generally southwest before joining the Tideway stretch of the River Thames at Brentford. The River Brent – the Old English meaning is 'sacred waters' – was named by the Celts, but it isn't known whether the original ford at Brentford was a crossing of the Brent or the Thames.

The Brent flows alongside the North Circular Road through Brent Park and under the Northern Line to Brent Cross and the Brent Reservoir. The reservoir – popularly called the Welsh Harp Reservoir after a pub that once stood nearby – has a feeder channel to the Grand Union Canal in Harlesden. From the reservoir the river flows through Neasden and Stonebridge, passing via an aqueduct under the Grand Union Canal (see Walk 7) in Alperton to Pitshanger Park in Perivale. From Perivale it continues south via the Brent Valley and Brent Lodge Parks to Hanwell – which is where the walk begins.

From Hanwell we follow the river along its final 4 miles (6½km), from Wharncliffe Viaduct to the foot of the Hanwell flight of locks, where it's joined by the main line of the Grand Union Canal. From here the Brent is canalised and navigable, flowing southeast along the western border of Brent River Park and Boston Manor Park, before navigating a number of locks and arriving in Brentford. Here we explore Brentford's restaurants, arts centre and museums, before heading to our final destination at Kew Bridge.

Hanwell flight of locks

Start Walking...

From Hanwell railway station take the tunnel under the railway line to Station Approach and go right and right again on Station Road. Follow the road back under the railway line and go left on Alwyne Road to **Alwyne Road Park** ❶. Follow the path through the park and turn left just after Manor Court Road to head for the magnificent 900ft (270m) **Wharncliffe Viaduct** ❷. Named after Lord Wharncliffe, chairman of Great Western Railway for which the viaduct was constructed in 1836-7, the viaduct still carries trains across the Brent valley at an elevation of 65ft (20m). It was Isambard Kingdom Brunel's first major structural project and was declared a listed building (Grade I) by Historic England in 1949 – one of the first buildings to receive this designation. The hollow cavities of its supporting piers are home to a colony of bats.

> ## Hanwell
>
> Located in the London borough of Ealing, the oldest written record of Hanwell was in 959AD when it was recorded as Hanewelle in pledge, when a Saxon called Alfwyn pawned his land to go on a pilgrimage. The name probably refers to a stream (*weille*) frequented by cocks (*hana*). By the time of the *Domesday Book* in 1086, Hanwell belonged to Westminster Abbey. The town owed its existence to the Uxbridge Road – then known as the Oxford Road – an important highway between Oxford and Tyburn in the 1700s, which had a number of coaching inns along its route.

Wharncliffe Viaduct

After going under the viaduct the path turns right and crosses over the River Brent, then continues south along the Brent River Park Walk (part of the Capital Ring route) under the A4020 Uxbridge Road, where **The Viaduct** ❸ pub, once an old coaching inn, is 50m along on the left. After around 500m the path emerges onto the towpath, here known as the Grand Union Canal Walk – off to the right is the **Old Lock-keeper's Cottage** ❹ – where you turn left to walk east. A short way along you pass **Hanwell Lock 97** ❺, aka the Bottom Lock, one of seven that make up the Hanwell Lock Flight, and it's just after this that the main line of the Grand Union Canal flows into the River Brent. There's a bridge here and, a few steps along, a signpost for the **Fox** ❻ on nearby Green Lane – a Victorian pub that's an excellent pitstop for a pint or lunch.

Back on the towpath, continue for another 500m to reach **Elthorne Park** ❼ which starts just after the bridge beneath Trumpers Way. The name dates back at least 1,000 years and was mentioned in the *Domesday Book* in 1086, although the park only officially opened in 1910 and

The Fox

Boston Manor House

is located on land leased from Lord Jersey, the owner of nearby Osterley Park. Spread over 10 acres (4ha), the park's layout includes lime and horse chestnut trees planted on the lawn, open lawns with an axial walk and floral displays. Elthorne Park abuts Elthorne Waterside (37 acres/15ha, aka the Elthorne Park Extension, part of Brent River Park) along the Brent, which was created in the '70s and is managed for nature conservation.

Near the end of the park the path crosses a footbridge, and here the river splits into two channels (forming an island) and passes the **Osterley Lock 98 ❽**. At the end of the 'island' you cross another footbridge – where the two channels of the river merge again – and continue along the canal walk passing under the M4 motorway. After another few hundred metres you go under a railway

line and arrive at **Boston Manor Playing Fields ❾**, which cover 32 acres (13ha) and are owned by London Playing Fields, a charity (est. 1890) that provides football, cricket and rugby pitches for local schools and clubs. Some 200m further on, the towpath crosses over the river and runs along its southern bank.

On the northern side of the river, Boston Manor Playing Fields border **Boston Manor Park ❿** (8am-dusk, see box), 20 acres (8ha) of beautiful parkland surrounding **Boston Manor House ⓫**. Grade I listed, the splendid Jacobean manor house dates from 1623; sadly, the house will be closed for two years from early 2019 to spring 2021 for restoration. Unfortunately, both the playing fields and park are blighted by the Boston Manor Viaduct which carries the M4, slicing the park in two.

Just beyond Boston Manor Park you pass a footbridge over the river and

Boston Manor Park

Situated on ground sloping gently down to the River Brent, the estate and house were built for Lady Mary Reade, a young widow who remarried not long after its completion. Her second husband was Sir Edward Spencer of Althorp, Northamptonshire, an ancestor of the late Diana, Princess of Wales. The estate was sold to Brentford Urban District Council in 1924, when the land became a public park. In addition to a lake with wildfowl and an island, there are ornamental lawns, herbaceous borders, a nature trail with a wildflower meadow and a 'secret' garden. Sports facilities include three tennis courts, a basketball court, soccer pitches and a bowling green, plus a large children's play area.

Boston Manor Park & M4 flyover

around 100m further on the path goes under the Great West Road (A4) and a railway line, before arriving at Brentford Basin and the **Brentford Gauging Lock**  . The lock is so-called because it was where the toll keeper measured (using a gauging rod) how high a boat sat out of the water in order to determine the amount of cargo it carried; this was used to calculate the toll to be paid to use the canal. The toll house (1911, Grade II listed) next to the lock contains a small museum. Cross over the lock to the island formed by the canal and river, keep to the right and cross the footbridge on the right, where you pass **Siracusa 13** , a dock-side restaurant serving pizzas and classic Italian fare. Continue along the path and down the steps to Brentford High Street, where the Thames, a popular Chinese restaurant, is on the left.

Turn right on the High Street and take the path on the left of the bridge to return to the Grand Union Canal Walk, where the canal is lined with boats. A bit further along on the opposite side of the river is **Syon Park 14** (200 acres/80ha), where splendid Syon Houses has been the home of the Percy family (the Dukes of Northumberland) since 1594.

After 500m or so, a footbridge takes you over the river to **Brentford Dock 15** (see box), a riverside development constructed on the site of the old dock. Turn left down some steps to continue along the waterside and after a few hundred metres you come to the **Thames Locks, Brentford 16** , a double lock that officially marks the end of the Grand Union Canal – the remaining few hundred metres of waterway to the Thames is the River Brent. Opposite the dock across the Thames are the

Brentford Dock

Brentford Dock – just to the south of the mouth of the River Brent and Grand Union Canal – was designed by Isambard Kingdom Brunel and built by the Great Western Railway (GWR); it opened in 1859 and was a major trans-shipment point between the railway and barges on the Thames. The dock closed in 1964 and was redeveloped in the '70s, and is now the Brentford Dock Estate and Marina.

celebrated **Royal Botanic Gardens, Kew 17** .

From Thames Lock walk up the steps and cross the river to Dock Road; turn left to return to the High Street, where you turn right. After a few hundred metres

Thames Locks, Brentford

you pass Lot's Ait (1.7 acres/0.7ha) and the larger **Brentford Ait 18** , two islands (aits or eyots) in the Thames. Lot's Ait is accessible via a footbridge at low tide and is home to a boat building company, while Brentford Ait (4.6 acres/2ha) is inaccessible by foot and is uninhabited today, but in the 18th century was home to a notorious pub called the Swan or Three Swans. It's covered in willows and alder planted in the '20s and is now a bird sanctuary with an important heronry.

Mighty Wurlitzer, Musical Museum

Facing Lot's Ait is the **Watermans Art Centre** ⑲, with a theatre and cinema, while opposite Brentford Ait is **Watermans**

London Museum of Water & Steam

This unusual museum (est. 1975) tells the story of London's water supply – from Roman times to the present day – and houses a magnificent collection of steam engines and diesel-powered water pumping machines. It's housed within the Georgian and Italianate buildings of the former Kew Bridge Pumping Station – opened in 1838 by the Grand Junction Waterworks Company – which supplied west Londoners with water for over 100 years until the engines were retired in 1944. The museum is home to the world's largest collection of Cornish beam engines, including the largest working beam engine, the spectacular Grand Junction 90 Engine, which pumped water for 98 years. It also features London's only operating steam railway and has a café and a pleasant garden for picnics. (See wateradnsteam.org.uk for more information.)

Park ⑳ – adjacent to the High Street – alongside which is a popular mooring site for houseboats (where a controversial new marina is planned).

At the end of the park, just across the high street, is the **Musical Museum** ㉑ (Tue, Fri-Sun, 10.30am-5pm, fee, musicalmuseum.co.uk). Founded in 1963 by Frank Holland (1910-1989), this unique, purpose-built museum contains one of the world's largest collections of automated (self-playing) musical instruments. From a tiny clockwork musical box to the 'Mighty Wurlitzer' concert organ, the collection embraces an impressive array of sophisticated reproducing pianos, pianolas, barrel organs, orchestrions, residence organs and violin players. Upstairs is a concert hall complete with an orchestra pit from which the Wurlitzer organ console (formerly installed at the Regal Cinema, Kingston-upon-Thames) rises to entertain you, just as it did in the '30s. The museum has a pleasant tea room and an interesting shop.

A little further along the High Street is another absorbing museum, the **London Museum of Water & Steam** ㉒ (Wed-Sun 10am-4pm, fee, see box). From the steam museum, continue along the High Street, passing the **Express Tavern** 23 – a good place to celebrate the walk's completion – to reach Kew Bridge railway station and the end of the walk. A few

Low tide at Brentford

6 **The Fox:** Highly-rated family-run pub in Green Lane, Hanwell, offering superb ales and above-average pub grub (Mon-Thu 11am-11pm, Fri-Sat 11am-11.30pm, Sun noon-11pm, £).

13 **Siracusa:** Italian restaurant opposite Brentford Lock serving stone-baked pizzas and classic Italian fare (Mon-Fri noon-3pm/5-10pm, Sat noon-10pm, closed Sun, £).

23 **Express Tavern:** A traditional CAMRA award-winning pub close to Kew Bridge (Sun-Thu 11am-11pm, Fri-Sat 11am-midnight, £).

hundred metres south is **Kew Bridge** **24**, the third bridge on the site, designed by Sir John Wolfe Barry and Cuthbert A. Brereton, and constructed in 1903.

Kew Bridge

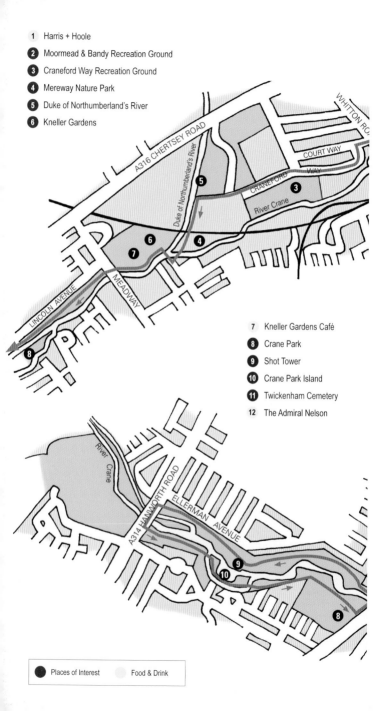

1 Harris + Hoole
2 Moormead & Bandy Recreation Ground
3 Craneford Way Recreation Ground
4 Mereway Nature Park
5 Duke of Northumberland's River
6 Kneller Gardens

7 Kneller Gardens Café
8 Crane Park
9 Shot Tower
10 Crane Park Island
11 Twickenham Cemetery
12 The Admiral Nelson

Places of Interest   Food & Drink

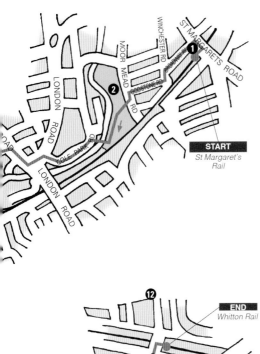

START
St Margaret's Rail

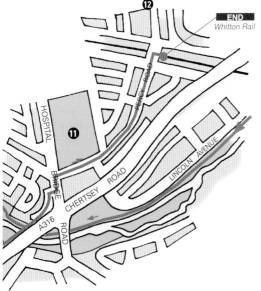

END
Whitton Rail

River Crane

Distance: 5½ miles (9 km)
Terrain: easy
Duration: 3 hours
Start: St Margarets rail
End: Whitton rail
Postcode: TW1 2LH

RIVER CRANE

The River Crane – also known as the 'Powder Mill River' after its former gunpowder mills – is a tributary of the River Thames, flowing 8½ miles (13½km) in west London from Minet Country Park in Hayes (Hillingdon) to the Thames at Isleworth. Just south of the park the river is fed by its 16-mile (26km) tributary, Yeading Brook, and passes under the main line of the Grand Union Canal, 100m west of Bull's Bridge where the western end of the Grand Union's Paddington Arm begins.

From Hayes the river runs south through Cranford Park and Cranford, along the eastern side of Heathrow Airport past the Balancing Reservoir – where the Duke of Northumberland's River, a tributary and distributary of the River Colne, joins the Crane – and Hounslow Heath. It then turns gradually east through Crane Park and Kneller Gardens in Twickenham, and continues to Isleworth where it flows into the Thames.

This walk commences at St Margarets station in East Twickenham. We join the Crane in the Moormead and Bandy Recreation Ground and follow the river upstream through Twickenham, skirting Craneford Way Recreation Ground and Kneller Gardens. The final section follows the river through beautiful Crane Park – which has a huge variety of habitats, including woodland, reed bed, ditches, ponds and river, along with a delightful nature reserve with a calming wilderness feel – before returning along the southern edge of the park and then heading to Whitton for the journey home.

Wild flowers, Crane Park

River Crane

Kneller Gardens

Start Walking...

From St Margarets railway station go left along St Margarets Road and turn left on Broadway Avenue, where there's a **Harris + Hoole** 1 café on the corner if you fancy breakfast or a brew. At the end of the avenue, go left on Winchester Road, right on Godstone Road and cross over Moor Mead Road to enter **Moormead and Bandy Recreation Ground** 2. Cross the park via the diagonal path where you have your first glimpse of the River Crane, which forms the park's western perimeter. In the southwest corner take the footpath leading to Cole Park Road which follows the river to London Road;

Duke of Northumberland's River

Consisting of two sections of artificial waterway in southwest London, the river can be described as a distributary of the Colne and a tributary of the Crane; it's also a distributary of the Crane and a tributary of the Thames. The Duke of Northumberland's River comprises separate eastern and western sections constructed in the 16th century to provide water for mills in Isleworth producing flour and calico. The eastern section diverts water from the River Crane alongside Kneller Gardens in Twickenham, and then flows northeast past two rugby grounds – The Stoop, home of the Harlequins, and Twickenham Stadium – and through Isleworth (where it originally powered a mill), then onwards to supply the fish ponds in the Duke of Northumberland's estate at Syon Park.

cross over to the junction with Whitton Road and walk north past a row of shops. Take the first left on Court Way and go left again along Craneford Way, which swings west to run along the top of **Craneford Way Recreation Ground** 3. Cross the playing fields diagonally and follow the path west along the river to the southwest corner where it meets the River Crane Walk.

The walk continues west alongside an industrial park, parallel with a railway line, and goes left through a tunnel, from where it crosses **Mereway Nature Park** 4, a small nature reserve. Just before the River Crane, turn right along the path that crosses over the **Duke of Northumberland's River** 5 (see box) via the Kingfisher Bridge to enter **Kneller Gardens** 6. Opened in 1931, the popular gardens are named after German artist Sir Godfrey Kneller (1646-1723), the leading portrait painter of his day, who lived in Whitton. The gardens contain pretty wildflower meadows in the spring and summer, and kingfishers and other water birds can be spotted along the rivers. The gardens also offer an abundance of sports facilities and relaxing **Kneller Gardens Café** 7 in the middle of the park.

Follow the path along the southern perimeter of Kneller Gardens parallel with

Hounslow Gunpowder Works

The gunpowder works opened in the 1760s and flourished into the 20th century before closing in 1926. It was reputed to have produced the finest black gunpowder in Europe. One of the constituents, charcoal, was produced from willow and alder, readily available along the river banks, while the river provided water power for the mills and transport for barges. Crane Park Island – now a nature reserve – was created to contain a mill pool of water to drive the mill machinery, remains of which can still be seen (including wheel pits and machine bases), along with various mill streams.

the River Crane, cross the Meadway and continue southwest along the path running beside the river to enter **Crane Park** ❽ (see box). The first section of path within the park runs along the tree-lined northern bank of the river and goes under two road bridges; thereafter the path becomes more densely wooded and the river is lined with weeping willows. Follow the path north of the river and after around 500m you arrive at the **Shot Tower** ❾

(Grade II listed), the only surviving building from the Hounslow Gunpowder Works (see box).

The Shot Tower was constructed in 1828 and is now a nature study and visitor centre (Sun, 1.30-4.30pm) with toilets. Shot towers were used to produce lead shot by pouring molten lead through a copper sieve from the top of the tower; as the lead fell it formed small round pellets, which cooled and hardened as they hit the water in a large tank at the bottom of the tower. However, it's now thought that the tower was either a windmill for recirculating water to power the mills or a watchtower to alert workers to fire hazard, rather than a shot tower. Near the Shot Tower is a bridge leading to **Crane Park Island** ❿ (see box opposite).

Continue along the path to Hanworth Road, where you go left and cross over the River Crane and take the southern path back along the river. The path loops around Crane Park Island and past a play area, before running alongside Great Chertsey Road (A316) and crossing over the river. Exit the park and follow the footpath along Crane Park Road to Hospital Bridge Road and cross over after around 150m to Percy Road, which runs past **Twickenham Cemetery** ⓫ and leads to Whitton railway station and the end of the walk. If you fancy a drink or

Crane Park

After the closure of the gunpowder works in 1926, the owner sold part of the site to Twickenham Council, which opened it as a public park in 1935. The lovely park is a wildlife haven and includes large areas of woodland, as well as pasture and riverbank. The 74-acre (20ha) linear park follows the course of the River Crane and is a Site of Metropolitan Importance for Nature Conversation with two Local Nature Reserves.

Shot Tower

some lunch, the High Street just beyond the station offers plenty of options – if you fancy a pint try **The Admiral Nelson** 12 pub at the far end.

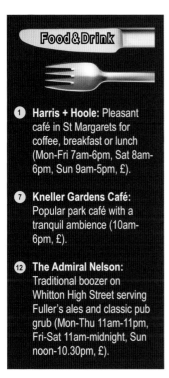

Food & Drink

1 **Harris + Hoole:** Pleasant café in St Margarets for coffee, breakfast or lunch (Mon-Fri 7am-6pm, Sat 8am-6pm, Sun 9am-5pm, £).

7 **Kneller Gardens Café:** Popular park café with a tranquil ambience (10am-6pm, £).

12 **The Admiral Nelson:** Traditional boozer on Whitton High Street serving Fuller's ales and classic pub grub (Mon-Thu 11am-11pm, Fri-Sat 11am-midnight, Sun noon-10.30pm, £).

Crane Park Island

The island is a nature reserve managed by the London Wildlife Trust, providing a home for many important and rare species, and is also an important place to learn about the River Crane as it flows downstream towards Isleworth. It contains a wide variety of vegetation – a rich mosaic of woodland, scrub, meadow, reed beds and river bank – and is home to a variety of wildlife, from darting damselflies and dragonflies to secretive foxes, noisy marsh frogs and rare water voles. Among the many bird species you can see here are kingfishers, grey heron, great spotted woodpeckers and treecreepers, while the river supports some 15 varieties of fish.

Crane Park Island

A2

CONINGTON RD

BROOKMILL ROAD

LEATHWELL RD

ARMOURY ROAD

THURSTON RD

LOAMPIT VALE

MOLESWORTH ST

MARSALA ROAD

LADYWELL ROAD

LEWISHAM HIGH ST

LADYWELL ROAD

1 Travelodge

2 Broadway Fields

3 Brookmill Park

4 Stephen Lawrence Centre

5 Elverson Road DLR station

6 Glass Mill Leisure Centre

7 River Quaggy

8 Cornmill Gardens

9 Lewisham Shopping Centre

10 Le Delice

11 Ladywell Fields

12 Old Swimming Baths

13 University Hospital Lewisham

14 Catford Bridge Railway Station

15 River Pool Linear Park

16 River Pool

17 The Railway Tavern

Places of Interest   Food & Drink

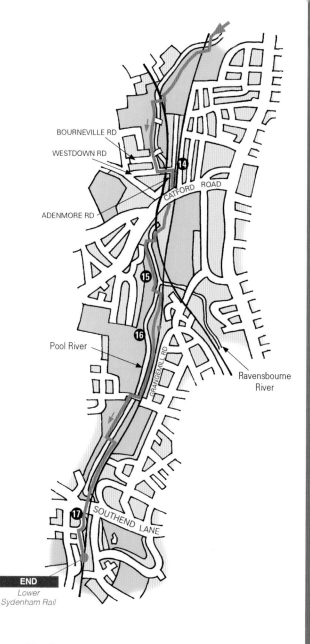

BOURNEVILLE RD

WESTDOWN RD

ADENMORE RD

14

CATFORD ROAD

15

16

Pool River

GRANGEMILL RD

Ravensbourne
River

17

SOUTHEND LANE

END
*Lower
Sydenham Rail*

WALK 13

River Ravensbourne

Distance: 4¾ miles (7½ km)

Terrain: easy

Duration: 2-3 hours

Start: Deptford Bridge rail/DLR

End: Lower Sydenham rail

Postcode: SE10 8EA

RIVER RAVENSBOURNE

The River Ravensbourne (11miles/17km) is a tributary of the River Thames that flows through southeast London, rising in Keston, four miles south of Bromley town centre. It flows into the Thames at Deptford where its tidal reach is known as Deptford Creek, one of the last surviving natural creeks in the UK. According to legend the Ravensbourne was named by Julius Caesar who spotted a raven flying above a drinking well at the source of the river; the well still exists and is known as Caesar's Well. At the time of the *Domesday Book* in 1086, eleven corn mills were recorded along the Ravensbourne.

The river has been modified over the past 150 years to allow for the building of railways, housing and flood prevention schemes, but it was never culverted (a fate that befell its neighbour, the River Peck, which can still be seen in Peckham Rye Park). This walk follows two-thirds of the route of the Waterlink Way (part of the National Cycle Network), a 7-mile (11¼ km) trail between Lower Sydenham and Deptford Creek.

Our walk begins at Deptford Bridge, just south of Deptford Creek, and follows the river upstream through Broadway Fields and Brookmill Park to Lewisham. We leave the river here and pick up the path again at Ladywell Fields, following it to Catford. Here we leave the Ravensbourne (which cannot be followed at this point) and continue along a tributary, the River Pool, to end our walk in Lower Sydenham.

River Ravensbourne

Start Walking…

Exit Deptford Bridge railway (or DLR station) onto the busy A2 road; the road is called Deptford Bridge at this point after the bridge over Deptford Creek. This was the site of the Battle of Deptford Bridge in 1497, the last battle of the Cornish Rebellion, a popular uprising by the people of Cornwall (who were still in open rebellion against Norman rule) in response to higher taxes imposed by Henry VII. The nearest decent coffee shops are in Deptford Broadway or Deptford High

Deptford Creek

Deptford

Situated between touristy Greenwich and rough-and-ready Bermondsey, Deptford – home to the first Royal Naval Dockyard founded by Henry VIII in 1513 (closed in the '60s) – has an atmosphere all its own, with a strong south London identity and quirky charm. Despite regeneration and a plethora of new bars, cafés and restaurants, the town has managed to retain its character and strong community vibe, and has become one of south London's most popular residential districts.

Street, although if you aren't too fussy you can refuel at the **Travelodge** ① just east of the station.

Take the footpath which runs between the river and the station, leading south to **Broadway Fields** ②. The park, which straddles both sides of the Ravensbourne River, opened in 1932 on a plot of land next to the Kent Water Works (see box on page 114). Walk along the eastern side of the river until,

after around 100m, the path crosses a bridge and continues parallel to Brookmill Road on its way through **Brookmill Park** ③. As you cross the river the **Stephen Lawrence Centre** ④ looms large on the left, an educational centre dedicated to improving opportunities for young black people, established in memory of murdered aspiring architecture student, Stephen Lawrence (1974-1993).

Formerly known as Ravensbourne Park, the linear Brookmill Park began life in 1880 as a small recreation ground near the Kent Water Works' reservoir, which drew water from the Ravensbourne to supply homes in Deptford and Greenwich. In the '20s, part of the (by then) disused reservoir was in-filled and added to the recreation

Stephen Lawrence Centre

Kent Water Works

Founded in 1701 as the Ravensbourne Water Company – one of the earliest water companies south of the Thames – the name was changed in 1809 when it was purchased by the Kent Water Works Company. Originally water was taken from the Ravensbourne, though later it was drawn from wells. The company provided water to Deptford, Lee, Greenwich, Lewisham and Rotherhithe, along with the town of Woolwich, the Royal Ordnance and Artillery Barracks, the Royal Arsenal, HM Dockyards and the Royal Observatory at Greenwich. After the Metropolis Water Act 1902 was passed, the Metropolitan Water Board took over the Kent Water Works Company in 1904. Thames Water still takes water from the site, but the reservoir has been covered and the course of the river much altered to accommodate flood prevention measures and the Docklands Light Railway.

ground, creating Brookmill Park. Nearby housing was destroyed during the Second World War and the cleared ground was added to the park, which re-opened in 1951 as Ravensbourne Park. During the Docklands Light Railway extension to Lewisham in the '90s, the river was rerouted (and straightened) and most of the park to the east of the river was appropriated for the DLR track, thus the

Ravensbourne's new channel became the eastern boundary of the park. The park was re-landscaped as a formal garden with a small lake (part of the former reservoir), pergolas, mature trees and flowerbeds. Covering 5 acres (2ha), with areas of marsh, water and grassland, some of which floods at high tide, the park is now an important nature conservation area.

Food & Drink

1. **Travelodge London Greenwich:** Close to Deptford Bridge railway and DLR stations, this is the nearest pit stop for coffee or breakfast (breakfast served Mon-Fri 7-10am, Sat-Sun 8-11am, £).

9. **Lewisham Shopping Centre:** A wide range of places to eat, including Costa Coffee, Greggs and an M&S café (Mon-Fri 9am-5.30pm, 8pm Thu, Sat 9am-6pm, Sun 11am-5pm, £).

10. **Le Delice:** Cakes, crepes and coffee in Ladywell village (Mon-Fri 7am-7pm, Sat 7am-6pm, Sun 8am-5.30pm, £).

17. **Railway Tavern:** Traditional local, offering standard pub fare (noon-11pm, £).

Brookmill Park

Brookmill Park is located in the district of St Johns, noted for its late 19th-century housing; it was constructed as Deptford New Town, and is now a conservation area. St Johns station was the site of one of Britain's worst railway disasters in 1957, when a steam express train ploughed into the rear of a standing train in dense fog, killing 90 people and injuring 176.

River Quaggy

The River Quaggy – the name probably comes from quagmire – is 11 miles (17km) in length and rises from two sources near Farnborough Hospital at Locksbottom (Bromley). In its lower reaches it's an urban river, but in its upper reaches, upstream of Sundridge Park, it's more natural and known as Kyd Brook.

At the end of the park, follow the path alongside the river until it crosses Elverson Road, passing **Elverson Road DLR station 5**; some 50m further on, cross back over the river and continue along its west bank. Just before the end of the path turn right to Armoury Road and cross the carpark to take the path leading under the railway to Thurston Road, where you go left. At the end go left on Rennell Street

(A20) and cross over to the **Glass Mill Leisure Centre 6**, then follow the path to the left of the centre (just before the railway bridge), which runs along the Ravensbourne. A short distance to the north (opposite Lewisham DLR station) the Ravensbourne merges with one of its tributaries, the delightfully named **River Quaggy 7** (see box).

The path leads along the river through **Cornmill Gardens 8**, where one of the Ravensbourne mills once stood. Opposite the gardens, you can turn left over the Ravensbourne to Molesworth Street and the **Lewisham Shopping Centre 9**. The centre, opened in 1977, is one of the largest in southeast London, covering 330,000ft² (30,650m²) and home to some 70 stores. It's a handy place for a pit stop, offering a choice of cafés

Cornmill Gardens

and fast-food outlets. Continue along the river to Waterway Avenue and turn right at the end into Smead Way and on to Elmira Street, where you go left. Take the second left on Marsala Road which leads south for some 500m to Algernon Road; turn left here, then left again to Ladywell Road and Ladywell Village. If you're peckish, just opposite is **Le Delice 10**, an excellent French patisserie/café.

Turn left on Ladywell Road and after around 100m take the path on the right to rejoin the Ravensbourne

Glass Mill Leisure Centre

Ladywell Fields

Running alongside the park on its eastern side is **University Hospital Lewisham** ⓭, on the site of an ancient workhouse. In 2007-2008 the river was split adjacent to the hospital and the smaller stream was allowed to follow its original meandering route through Ladywell Fields. Follow the path past the hospital, cross over the river and continue south to the last section of park, where the elevated railway crosses overhead. Pass under the railway bridge and follow the path of the river south, exiting the park on Bourneville Road. From here, go left on Westdown Road at the end and right on Adenmore Road. You're now in Catford, which takes its name from a ford where cattle crossed the Ravensbourne in Saxon times (or, alternatively, from wild cats that used to frequent the ford). The town has two railway stations serving different lines: Catford and, 100m to the east, **Catford Bridge Railway Station** ⓮. They were once separated by Catford Stadium (1932-2003), a historic greyhound racing venue, and the area (now redeveloped) is known as Catford Green.

Ladywell Fields

This popular park (54 acres/22ha) is a mile (1.6km) in length and home to a variety of mature trees, including hybrid black poplar and a rare surviving elm on the river bank, bearing a Great Trees of London plaque (denoting trees considered of importance to the capital). There's also a wide range of recreation facilities, including play areas, a skate park and ball courts, a bowling green and football pitch, plus a café.

---

as it flows along the eastern perimeter of **Ladywell Fields** ⓫ (see box). The name Ladywell comes from a medicinal well, reputed to be a cure for eye complaints. The well was first recorded here in 1472 and named after St Mary the Virgin ('our lady's well') – the parish church of St Mary the Virgin is next to the park. A short walk east of the park entrance, opposite Church Grove, is the red-brick **Old Swimming Baths** ⓬ (aka the Ladywell Playtower) constructed in 1884, complete with water tower. The public baths were designed in Gothic style by Wilson and Son and Thomas Aldwinkle, and consisted of first and second class swimming pools. Badly damaged by fire in 2005, the Grade II listed building is scheduled to be restored and brought back into public use.

River Pool Linear Park

At the end of Adenmore Road, cross the South Circular Road and follow the path along the road past Halfords and Wickes which leads under the railway line to enter the **River Pool Linear**

Park **15**. The path continues through the park alongside the Ravensbourne, crossing over the river after 50 metres and continuing for another 200m until the river takes a sharp turn to the east. From here it's no longer possible to navigate the Ravensbourne; instead continue south along the **River Pool 16** (see box). The path follows the river upstream, along a scenic linear route lined with native trees and shrubs, herbaceous planting, wild flowers and grassland, river bank and wetlands. The nature conservation area provides paths for walking or cycling along the river and for spotting flora and fauna as you head south to Sydenham.

At the southern end of the park, cross Southend Lane to Fambridge Close, past the **Railway Tavern** 17 – last chance saloon if you fancy a drink – and follow the footpath that leads left to Lower Sydenham railway station and the end of the walk.

River Pool

A tributary of the Ravensbourne, the River Pool (3 miles/5km) runs from New Beckenham – where it's formed in Cator Park by its tributaries, the River Beck and the Chaffinch Brook – to the Pool River Linear Park where it joins the Ravensbourne. For much of its length the river lies in a flood plain, the land on either side being utilised as sports grounds. At Sydenham the river flowed through the former 19th-century Bell Green gasworks site, where it was canalised and culverted below ground so as not to interfere with gas production. The creation of a park in recent years led to the river being rerouted in an open channel, designed to accommodate flood waters and reduce the impact of potential flooding downstream in Catford and Lewisham.

River Pool

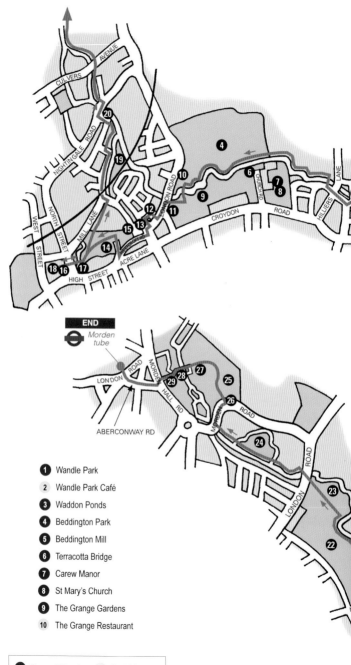

END

🚇 Morden tube

1. Wandle Park
2. Wandle Park Café
3. Waddon Ponds
4. Beddington Park
5. Beddington Mill
6. Terracotta Bridge
7. Carew Manor
8. St Mary's Church
9. The Grange Gardens
10. The Grange Restaurant

● Places of Interest　　● Food & Drink

WALK 14

Upper River Wandle

Distance: 8 miles (13 km)
Terrain: easy
Duration: 3-4 hours
Start: West Croydon rail
End: Morden tube
Postcode: CR0 2TA

UPPER RIVER WANDLE

The River Wandle (ca. 11 miles/18km) is a tributary of the River Thames in south London, rising from two sources in Waddon and Carshalton and flowing north to Wandsworth. Due to its length we have divided the Wandle into two walks: the Upper and Lower Wandle. This walk explores the more rural upper section of the Wandle, while the lower reaches, which reveal its more industrialised character, feature in Walk 15. In its industrial heyday the Wandle was Britain's hardest working – and most polluted – river, with as many as 90 mills along its banks. Today, this typical chalk stream has been cleaned up and revitalised, and is teeming with fish and other wildlife, and made accessible by the 12½-mile (20km) Wandle Trail.

This walk commences in Croydon from where we go west to Wandle Park, then southwest to Waddon Ponds. From here we follow the river west to Beddington Park and the Grove in Carshalton, before heading north via a series of beautiful parks, from Wilderness Island to Morden Hall Park, ending the walk at Merton tube station.

Wandle Park, Croydon

Start Walking...

After leaving West Croydon railway station, cross over London Road to Derby Road and take the first left to Clarendon Road. At the end, turn left onto Pitlake and follow the road as it curves right under Roman Way, then take the second left on Westfield Road which leads to **Wandle Park 1** . There are two Wandle Parks – you visit the other one in Colliers Wood on **Walk 15** – and at 21 acres (8.5ha), this is the larger of the two. Follow the footpath anticlockwise and soon after you pass **Wandle Park Café 2** , you catch your first glimpse of the River Wandle on the

Beddington Park

This glorious park was originally part of a deer park attached to Carew Manor, an important country mansion. The *Domesday Book* of 1086 mentions two Beddington estates, which were united by Nicholas Carew in 1381. The family reached its zenith in the Tudor period, when the park occupied most of the land between today's Mitcham Common, Beddington Lane, Croydon Road and London Road. The park is now divided into several sections, covering 94 acres (38ha) in total, all linked by the Wandle.

Waddon Ponds

right – it was restored to the surface here in 2012. Exit the park in the southwest corner, over the tramway to Vicarage Road; walk to the end and turn right on Waddon Road which leads to Purley Way. Cross to Mill Lane, where **Waddon Ponds 3** are 100m along on the left.

The springs which feed Waddon Ponds (8½ acres/3.4ha) support a variety of aquatic life and waterfowl. Most of the area is given over to ornamental water gardens with weeping willows trailing their drooping branches in the water. There's a trail around the ponds, although you continue west across the top of the ponds. Take the bridleway to the left of Mill Lane, signposted Wandle Trail, and after around

200m you come to the first (small) section of **Beddington Park 4** (see box), where you see the Wandle in all its glory.

Continue along the bridleway south of the river and cross over opposite Lavington Road to Richmond Green, turning left to follow the river's northern bank. When the road swings right, continue straight ahead along the path to Kingston Gardens and Wandle Road. One course of the river goes straight ahead, but you turn left on Wandle Road and after 75m go right on Bridges Lane. Opposite is the old **Beddington Mill 5** , a flour mill owned by the Carew family; it burnt down in the late 19th century and was replaced by the current building (now flats). A short way

Beddington Mill

Carew Manor

Grade I listed Carew Manor was the home of the Carews of Beddington for 500 years. The Great Hall, which dates from around 1500, survives from the original house and boasts a splendid hammer-beam roof, a collection of fine period furniture, antiques and works of art. In the grounds are part of the orangery, built in the early 18th century by Sir Francis Carew, and an early 18th-century dovecote. The Manor was previously home to the Royal Female Orphanage (1866-1968) and now houses council offices and Carew Academy.

the river and you'll see the **Terracotta Bridge** ❻ 100m along on your left. It was built by Watcombe Pottery (in Torquay, Devon) for Canon Bridges, Rector of Beddington, at the end of the 19th century. The wealthy clergyman had acquired the park in 1859 when the last of the Carew family was forced to sell the estate to pay his gambling debts. You can take a short detour south, over the bridge, to see **Carew Manor** ❼ (see box), once a medieval moated house. Alongside the manor is **St Mary's Church** ❽ (Grade II* listed), a handsome 14th-century flint parish church.

Return to the Terracotta Bridge and follow the Wandle as it wends its way across Beddington Park – past a small stone bridge and through a copse – and cross over the main path to **The Grange Gardens** ❾. Adjacent to the park, the gardens (44 acres/18ha) contain a variety of features, including a beautiful ornamental garden on the north side of Mill Pond created by Alfred Smee FRS, surgeon to the Bank of England, who purchased the site in the 1860s. In 1935, the house and grounds were acquired by the then borough of Beddington and Wallington and turned into a public park. The house is now home to **The Grange Restaurant** ❿ , a good choice for lunch.

Follow the path along the top of the Mill Pond and cross over the small bridge, which leads to a car park. Head south,

along Bridges Lane take the footpath on the right, signposted Beddington Park, that runs alongside the river, and cross over Hilliers Lane to Guy Road. After around 100m turn right across the bridge – where two arms of the river meet – and go left and follow the track through the second section of Beddington Park with the river on your left.

After a few hundred metres the path takes a sharp turn to the right, crossing the river and leading to Mallinson Road; just before you reach the road go left and follow the path along the wall until you cross the river again. The rough path continues diagonally across an open space to a car park, where you follow the road round to the left (past some cottages) and turn right to cross the Wandle once again and enter the main section of Beddington Park. Head west along

St Mary's Church

Carshalton Ponds

crossing **Manor Garden** 11 and Derek Avenue to walk down Lakeside and turn left into Quinton Close. Cross over London Road and follow the path and walk anticlockwise around **Elms Pond** 12 to Butter Hill, where you go left past the **Rose & Crown** 13 and right on Westcroft Road. This leads to **Grove Park** 14, aka the Grove. Turn right and take the path parallel to Westcroft Road, past the **Westcroft Leisure Centre** 15 and left along the bottom perimeter of the park, passing the bowling green, café and toilets. The southwest corner of the Grove abuts beautiful **Carshalton Ponds** 16, from where one source of the Wandle flows north through the park. The springs and ponds date back centuries (there was an early Saxon settlement here).

From the Grove, cross over the 18th-century **Leoni Bridge** 17, a white Portland stone bridge designed by the Italian architect Giacomo Leoni – which spans the link between the Wandle and the lower pond – and cross over North Street to Honeywood Walk. At the western end of the upper pond is the fascinating **Honeywood Museum** 18 (see box). Walk back across the Leoni Bridge and follow the path north along the river – passing the footbridge on the left where there's a lovely cascade – and go left at the junction. Cross over the river and head right along the path that follows the river up to Papermill Close. Another path links the Close to Mill Lane, which then follows the river to River Gardens and **Wilderness Island** 19. This is where the Croydon and Carshalton arms of the River Wandle meet, although only part of it is a genuine island. Dotted with ponds, it's now a nature reserve and provides a range of wildlife habitats.

Take the path on the right opposite 24 River Gardens to continue alongside the Wandle as it heads north and then

Honeywood Museum

This Grade II listed museum is Sutton borough's heritage centre and local history museum, occupying a handsome 17th-century building on the banks of Carshalton's scenic ponds. After being purchased by the local council in the late '30s, the building fell into disrepair, before being refurbished in 1990. The collection contains over 6,000 items – mainly from the 19th and 20th centuries – representing the history of the River Wandle and local communities. (For information see friendsofhoneywood.co.uk.)

Watermeads Nature Reserve

west. This brings you to **Claudio Funari's Community Garden** ⑳ at the end of The Causeway, where you turn right to Hackbridge Road. Turn right again, and just after you cross the river, cross over and take the path on the left (opposite Restmor Way). Soon after the river splits again and you follow the right-hand channel along its right-hand bank, crossing over Culvers Avenue, until some 300m further on the two arms of the Wandle join up again just before **Watercress Park** ㉑. The park is a reminder of the Wandle Valley's agricultural past;

watercress grew naturally here for centuries, before the industry went into decline due to pollution in the latter 19th century. At the north of the park, cross over the river and continue along the path, which leads past the trading estate and over a stream (not the Wandle) before emerging on to Middleton Road, where you cross over to Watermead Lane.

After passing some cottages, at the end of the lane the footpath resumes alongside the river and **Poulter Park** ㉒ (see box), which is one of the Wandle's most attractive settings. There are a number of weirs and a man-made waterfall and, after a loop in the river, an

Ravensbury Park

inlet where you cross over the waterway and continue along the river through the beautiful **Watermeads Nature Reserve** ㉓, owned by the National Trust. At the end of the reserve, cross London Road and follow the path along the river to **Ravensbury Park** ㉔, where the Wandle briefly splits into two channels once again – the path is down the middle – before running along the park's southern boundary. In the 13th century this was part of Ravensbury Manor and in the 17th-18th centuries it was the location of a snuff mill. First opened to the public in 1930, this 17-acre (7ha) park is now a Local Nature Reserve with extensive woodland and a range of wildlife habitats.

Poulter Park

Poulter Park (50 acres/20.5ha) is the home ground of the Croydon Camogie Club and the Tooting and Mitcham Community Sports Club. It's named after Reginald Poulter, a local architect who was instrumental in getting the site declared a public park in 1925. The rough path along the river is being cleaned up to make it safer, but its unkempt look only adds to its charm, although you need to take care, particularly when walking with children.

Food & Drink

2 **Wandle Park Café:** Pleasant café with outside seating run by a local social enterprise (9.30am-4pm, £).

10 **The Grange Restaurant:** Restaurant in Beddington Park offering a range of cuisines, from continental to Indo-Chinese (020-8773 8195, lunch noon-2.30pm, Sun noon-4pm, £).

29 **Potting Shed Café:** Homemade cake and lunches by the river in Morden Hall Park (9am-5/6pm, £).

At the end of the park you emerge onto Morden Road and turn right to visit **Morden Hall Park** **25** (unrestricted), which you enter just before the **Surrey Arms** **26**. Follow the main path around to the left (briefly skirting the Wandle) and just after the path crosses a stream take the fork on the left and follow it past the **Rose Garden** **27** and Morden Cottage, over the Wandle and past the **Snuff Mill** **28**. A little further on is the **Potting Shed Café** 29 , where you can get a well-earned cup of tea. From the café return to the main path and exit the park on Morden Hall Road. Cross over to Aberconway Road and walk to the end to reach Morden tube station.

Morden Hall Park

1 Morden Hall Park
2 Potting Shed Café
3 Garden Centre
4 Stable Yard
5 Snuff Mill
6 White Bridge
7 Morden Hall
8 Morden Hall Park Wetlands
9 Deen City Farm
10 Pickle Ditch
11 Merton Abbey Mills
12 Wandle Heritage Centre
13 Kiss Me Hardy Wacky Warehouse
14 Wandle Park
15 Wandle Meadow Nature Park
16 Garratt Park
17 The Wandle of Earlsfield
18 King George's Park

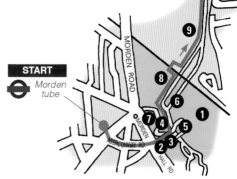

19 Nuffield Health Club
20 Southside Wandsworth
21 Bell Lane Creek
22 Bamford Community Gardens
23 The Alma

Places of Interest   Food & Drink

SMUGGLERS WAY

SWANDON WAY

River Thames

THE CAUSEWAY

22

23

21

END
*Wandsworth
Town Rail*

WANDSWORTH HIGH ST

20

18

ROAD

14

13

KIMBER ROAD

19

18

17

GARRATT LANE

PENWITH ROAD

16

DURNSFORD ROAD

WEIR ROAD

WALK 15

Lower River Wandle

Distance: 6½ miles (10½ km)

Terrain: easy

Duration: 3 hours

Start: Morden tube

End: Wandsworth Town rail

Postcode: SM4 5AZ

LOWER RIVER WANDLE

The River Wandle is a tributary of the River Thames which flows through south London. It's around 11 miles (18km) in length and rises from two sources west of Croydon – Waddon and Carshalton – before flowing north to Wandsworth. Due to its length we have divided the Wandle into two walks. The more rural section of the upper Wandle is explored in Walk 14, while this walk takes in its working, more urban segment, the lower Wandle.

The river has been well used since Roman times and was heavily industrialised in the 18th and 19th centuries, when it was one of the most polluted rivers in England. It was used to power up to 90 waterwheels, of which only a few survive, such as at Merton Abbey Mills, which used to produce paper, print and tapestries. The history of the river is told in the Wandle Industrial Museum (see wandle.org) in Mitcham.

The walk commences in beautiful Morden Hall Park, before heading north to Merton Abbey Mills and the Wandle Heritage Centre, and Wandle Park in Colliers Wood. From here we continue north, via the Wandle Meadow Nature Park and Garratt Park, to lovely King George's Park in Wandsworth, before arriving at Bell Lane Creek and the river's convergence with the Thames.

Morden Hall Park

Start Walking...

Exit from Morden tube station, cross London Road and walk along Aberconway Road to Morden Hall Road. Opposite is the entrance to **Morden Hall Park** ➊ (unrestricted, see box) via green double gates; the free car park is 100m further along on the left. Follow the path with the water channel on your left, part of a river-fed moat around Morden Hall. (The river has many channels and culverts in the park, both for decorative and practical reasons, including the powering of waterwheels.) On your right is the **Potting Shed Café** ➋ and the **Garden Centre** ➌.

Morden Hall Park

A tranquil former deer park, Morden Hall is one of the few estates to survive from those that lined the Wandle during its industrial heyday. It was home to the Garth family from the 16th century onwards, although the current house dates from the mid-18th century. In 1873, the estate was purchased by tobacco merchant Gilliat Hatfeild, who created much of the current park. His son Gilliat Edward Hatfeild (1864-1941), a bachelor, left the estate to the National Trust on his death. Today, it covers 125 acres (50ha), encompassing Morden Hall, its stable yard, pretty Morden Cottage and a number of old farm buildings.

Snuff Mill

Continue along the path past the **Stable Yard** ➍ on the left, now an energy-efficient eco building housing a visitor centre, gallery, second-hand bookshop and café. Next on the right is the former **Snuff Mill** ➎ which closed in 1922 and is now a learning centre.

Ahead, the old water mill is still in situ on the Wandle but is no longer in operation; look for the eel pass on the left side of the wheel that allows eels to navigate the river. Go left just after the Snuff Mill and walk along the river for around 100m to the famous **White Bridge** ➏ – a favourite spot for playing pooh sticks and posing for wedding photos. Look to the left to see a second bridge leading to **Morden Hall** ➐ (see box on page 130).

From the White Bridge follow the path northwest, where it crosses two small wooden bridges over two parallel channels of the Wandle. Turn right after the second bridge and follow the dragonfly signpost to the lush **Wetlands** ➑, home to a rich variety of wildlife, including

White Bridge

Morden Hall

Built between 1750 and 1765 within a moated enclosure created from the Wandle, the hall was home to the Garth family for generations, and later to tobacco merchant Gilliat Hatfeild. During the First World War it was a military hospital, and more recently, a restaurant and wedding venue.

one of the closest heronries to central London. After around 200m the path goes over a boardwalk, which zigzags its way north. On a platform in the middle of the boardwalk there are benches and an elevated viewing platform, where notices provide information regarding what you might see – a kingfisher, egret or heron, if you're lucky.

Just after the end of the boardwalk take the path to the right over the Tramlink line – take care when crossing – and follow it round to the right, past a large warehouse, where it continues along the Wandle. After around 400m you come to **Deen City Farm** ❾ (10am-4.30pm, closed Mondays), which has a café, farm shop, small animal enclosures and a riding school. Continue along the driveway past the farm on the bank of the Wandle and cross over Windsor Avenue, where the route continues as a footpath. Around 100m further up on the right is the **Pickle Ditch** ❿, which follows the old course of the Wandle in a looping arc. A short distance past the ditch cross a bridge on your right to **Merton Abbey Mills** ⓫ (see box), which houses a range of

restaurants, cafés, pubs, shops, weekend market and a theatre.

Follow the path through the buildings – past the **Wandle Heritage Centre** ⓬ (Sat-Sun 10am-5pm) and William Morris pub on the left – and cross back over the Wandle, then go right to continue along the river. The path leads under Merantun Way and crosses Station Road, where the Wandle arcs to the right before running parallel to Merton High Street; it was along this stretch just north of the river that textile designer (writer and social activist) William Morris had his works in the 1880s – the location is shown by a plaque. Just before you reach the High Street, cross over the river and head left along the path opposite Sainsbury's. A bit further along you cross the Pickle Ditch – just before it rejoins the Wandle – and follow the path round to the right, past the **Kiss Me Hardy Wacky Warehouse** ⓭ play centre, to reach Merton High Street.

Cross over the High Street and turn left for **Wandle Park** ⓮ (see box opposite) – not to be confused with a

Merton Abbey Mills

The mills, now a retail centre, take their name from Merton Priory, an Augustinian monastery established in the early 12th century. The idyllic riverside setting was the site of the Arthur Liberty silk printing works from 1904 until the '70s. Today, the waterwheel (dating from 1885) is one of the only fully working Victorian wheels in the country, and the only one driven by water power.

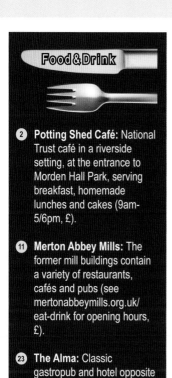

2 **Potting Shed Café:** National Trust café in a riverside setting, at the entrance to Morden Hall Park, serving breakfast, homemade lunches and cakes (9am-5/6pm, £).

11 **Merton Abbey Mills:** The former mill buildings contain a variety of restaurants, cafés and pubs (see mertonabbeymills.org.uk/eat-drink for opening hours, £).

23 **The Alma:** Classic gastropub and hotel opposite Wandsworth Town station (Mon-Fri 7am-midnight, Sat 8am-midnight, Sun 8am-10.30pm, £-££).

Wandle Park

Wandle Park (8am/9am-dusk) was the site of Wandle Bank House, built in 1791 by James Perry (1756-1821), owner of Merton Mill and also the owner and editor of the *Morning Chronicle*. The 11-acre (4.5ha) park contains the former millpond, grassed areas and woodland with some ancient trees. The house was demolished in 1962.

---

park of the same name in Croydon (see **Walk 14**) – where the Wandle forms the park's western boundary. Follow the path north through the park, over the former millpond, and cross the bridge over the river in the northwest corner to Wandle Bank. At the end of Wandle Bank (on the right) is the former Merton Mill, now converted to apartments. Originally a flour mill, it was adapted to leather production in 1905 and purchased by Connolly's Limited, who supplied leather to the cream of Britain's car manufacturers, including Rolls-Royce and Bentley. Sadly, the company ceased trading in 2002 after more than 125 years.

Go right on Bygrove Road, then immediately left on Bewley Street which follows the river, and after some 150m cross the bridge over the river to **Wandle Meadow Nature Park** **15**. Laid out over 10 acres (4ha) on the site of the former Wandle Valley Sewage Works, this linear park is a Local Nature Reserve with a mixture of habitats and abundant plant and wildlife. Follow the path through the park, over North Road, to its eastern edge, where it goes through a tunnel under the railway line and joins Mead Path, part of the Wandle Trail. This was the site of the Surrey Iron Railway, a horse-drawn plateway linking Wandsworth and Croydon via Mitcham (all then located in Surrey). The railway opened in 1802 but was only briefly successful and closed in 1846.

Wandle Meadow Nature Park

Walk 15

From the railway line the path follows the eastern edge of the park along the river for around 1km to Plough Lane, where Wimbledon Football Club (see box) had their ground from 1912-1991. Cross the bridge on Plough Lane and continue north along the path that now runs west of the river.

Bell Lane Creek

The path continues along a pretty stretch of river lined with trees – which conceal the surrounding industrial parks – for around 600m to **Garratt Park** ⑯, a tranquil green space with picnic tables, a children's playground, sports facilities, and allotments along the eastern riverbank. At the north end of the park the riverside path terminates at Trewint Street where you go right over the river, left on Summerley Street

and left again on Garratt Lane. Continue under the railway bridge, past Earlsfield railway station, and turn left on Penwith Road, where **The Wandle of Earlsfield** ⑰ pub is on the opposite corner. Follow Penwith Road for some 500m and turn right on Acuba Road. At the end, enter glorious **King George's Park** ⑱ (see box opposite).

Follow the path northeast across the park to its wooded eastern edge, where it follows the Wandle past the **Nuffield Health Club** ⑲ and the Kimber Skatepark and across Kimber Road. A short way along, the path veers left, away from the river, and follows the edge of the park, before heading north. Take the path on the right, just past Dynamic Sounds, which runs northeast crossing the river to join Mapleton Road. Turn left onto Garratt Lane and head north, past the **Southside Wandsworth** ⑳ shopping centre on the left (the river runs 'through' the shopping centre, where it's culverted) to Wandsworth High Street, where you go left. After 50m you cross back over the Wandle and go right on Wandsworth Plain to Armoury Way (A3), where you turn right and go left on Dormay Street, then immediately right along The Causeway, following the river once again.

After a short distance the road crosses over a bridge to The Spit – an island formed by the Wandle in the east and **Bell Lane Creek** ㉑ to the west. Continue

The Alma, Wandsworth

north on The Causeway to the cross path. The left-hand path crosses over a bridge over Bell Lane Creek and continues 150m north to where the Wandle flows into the Thames. This is where you take your leave of the Wandle. Follow the path on the right over the Wandle to Smugglers Way, passing B&Q on the right. At the end of the street cross over busy Swandon Way (A217) at the lights to Old York Road, passing **Bramford Community Gardens** **22** on your left, and follow the road round to Wandsworth Town railway station – and the end of the walk. If you're peckish or fancy a drink, opposite the station is **The Alma** 23 , a classic Young's gastropub and hotel.

King George's Park

Opened in 1923 by George V, after whom it's named, this beautiful linear park (55 acres/22ha) is around 770m long (north-south) and 120m wide, with the Wandle running along its eastern boundary. The park contains formal and ornamental gardens, an ecology site, lake and riverside walks, a play area and adventure playground, sports pitches, a leisure centre, bowling green and tennis courts.

The Wandle, Wandsworth

RIVER Thames

ROTHERHITHE
TUNNEL

SALTER ROAD

POOLMANS STREET

BRUNEL ROAD

SURREY

QUAYS ROAD

START & END
Rotherhithe Rail

BEDRIFF ROAD

BRUNSWICK QUAY

FINLAND STREET

ROPE STREET

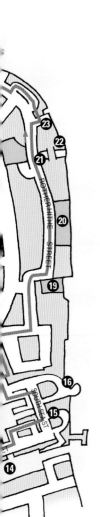

1 Brunel Museum
2 Mayflower Pub
3 Ventilation Shaft
4 Bascule Bridge
5 Surrey Water
6 Albion Channel
7 Canada Water
8 Leadbelly's Bar & Kitchen
9 Canada Water Library
10 Surrey Quays Shopping Centre
11 Greenland Dock
12 Redcliff Road Bridge
13 Surrey Docks Watersports Centre
14 South Dock Marina
15 Swing Footbridge
16 Curlicue
17 Norway Dock
18 The Moby Dick
19 Surrey Docks Farm
20 Durand's Wharf
21 Columbia Wharf
22 Nelson Dock Pier
23 The Blacksmiths Arms
24 Lavender Pond Nature Reserve
25 St Paul's Sports Ground
26 The Salt Quay Pub
27 Swan Road Mosaic Mural
28 The Brunel

● Places of Interest   ● Food & Drink

Rotherhithe Peninsula

WALK 16

ROTHERHITHE PENINSULA

Distance: 4½ miles (7¼ km)

Terrain: easy

Duration: 2-3 hours

Start/End: Rotherhithe rail

Postcode: SE16 4LF

Rotherhithe – the name is Anglo Saxon in origin and means 'landing place for cattle' or 'sailor haven' – is located in the borough of Southwark in southeast London. It has a long connection to the sea, as a port and home to a tight-knit community of shipbuilders and sailors, with shipyards from Elizabethan times until the mid-20th century. Its 'High Street' – Rotherhithe Street – is a rare complete 18th-century village, full of atmosphere and history, now a conservation area.

Rotherhithe Peninsula was the heartland of the Surrey Commercial Docks – comprising ten docks or timber ponds and the Surrey basin, extending to some 300 acres (121ha) – so-called because historically the area was the most north-eastern settlement in the county of Surrey. The only commercial docks south of the river,

Surrey Docks, 19th century

Surrey Docks closed in the '70s and the area was redeveloped in the '80s and early '90s as a residential district with a mix of warehouse conversions and new-build developments, renamed Surrey Quays. Today, the former docklands are part of a vast regeneration area, and while most have been in-filled, there are constant reminders of its maritime heritage. The pleasant marinas, wildlife reserves and new homes clustered around the Thames are worlds apart from Rotherhithe's industrial heritage but lend the area a unique charm.

The walk commences at Rotherhithe station and visits the fascinating Brunel Museum before heading east along Rotherhithe Street and south along Surrey Water to Canada Water in the heart of the old docks. From here we walk around Greenland Dock and turn north to rejoin Rotherhithe Street, visiting Surrey Docks Farm, Durand's Wharf and Lavender Pond, before heading west back along the Thames to our starting point.

Rotherhithe Peninsula

Start Walking...

From Rotherhithe railway station go left on Brunel Road and left again down Railway Avenue, where on the left just before the end is the **Brunel Museum** ❶ (see box); one of London's best small museums, it also has an excellent café. Just past the museum is the famous Rotherhithe Street – which runs for over 1½ miles (2½km) from just west of the **Mayflower Pub** ❷ to Elgar Street in east Rotherhithe. The pub, just a short walk west along Rotherhithe Street, is named after the Founding Fathers' ship that set sail for the New World from the pub's wharf in 1620.

Turn right on Rotherhithe Street and go left opposite Swan Road to follow the Thames Path for a brief stretch before returning to Rotherhithe Street. A bit

The Mayflower

further along is a circular red-brick building (largely hidden by a block of flats) that's a **Ventilation Shaft** ❸ for the Rotherhithe Tunnel (A101) running beneath the Thames – there's a twin on the opposite side of the river in King Edward VII Memorial Park. The road tunnel opened in 1908 and is 4,862ft (1.48km) long, connecting Rotherhithe (the entrance is adjacent to Brunel Road in Rotherhithe) with Limehouse on the north bank of the Thames.

Brunel Museum

This intriguing museum (fee, 10am-5pm) pays homage to three generations of the legendary Brunel engineering family: Sir Marc Isambard Brunel (1769-1849), his son Isambard Kingdom Brunel (1806-1859) – widely considered to be Britain's greatest ever engineer – and Isambard's second son, Henry Marc Brunel (1842-1903), also a civil engineer. It sits above the Thames Tunnel – built 1825-1843 and the first passenger tunnel under a navigable river – and includes the Brunel Engine House, where steam engines pumped water from the tunnel, and the stunning Grand Entrance Hall, described by Victorians as the Eighth Wonder of the World. A permanent exhibition tells the story of the tunnel. (For more information see brunel-museum.org.uk.)

Just after the ventilation shaft is one of the former entrances to Surrey Docks, marked by the **Bascule Bridge** ❹. Its massive red girders span a lock that once allowed sea-going ships access to the docks, but it's now out of action. Just before the bridge, follow the path on the right that runs alongside the waterway and across Salter Road to **Surrey Water** ❺. Then continue south along the **Albion Channel** ❻, which was created along the

Surrey Water

eastern side of the former Albion Dock, and links Canada and Surrey Waters. The channel flows under Poolmans Street and swings to the right past a plethora of new developments until arriving at Surrey Quays Road and **Canada Water** ❼ (see box). Turn right to cross the channel to Deal Porters Square, where there's a daily street food market (10am-8pm), or **Leadbelly's Bar & Kitchen** ❽ if you fancy a coffee.

Canada Water

The only body of fresh water in London's Docklands, this lake and wildlife refuge occupies the northern third of the original Canada Dock – and is also the name of the area which surrounds it. It was mainly used by ships from Canada, hence the name.

The imposing building to the north of Canada Water is **Canada Water Library** ❾; designed by Piers Gough, it resembles part of an inverted pyramid,

with a popular ground floor café and the library above. The cutting-edge public library combines with Canada Water Theatre to host theatre, music, dance, comedy, literature and community events. From the library walk around Canada Water, crossing back over the Albion Channel to take the Maritime Street path along its eastern side (past the Decathlon store). Turn right on Surrey Quays Road and walk south, past the Odeon Cinema and Hollywood Bowl ten-pin bowling centre on the left and the rear of **Surrey Quays Shopping Centre** ❿ on the right.

At the end of Surrey Quays Road go left at the roundabout to Redriff Road and then almost immediately right along the footpath (opposite the zebra crossing) to Brunswick Quay – where it becomes eerily peaceful – and go right along the western edge of **Greenland Dock** ⓫ (see box opposite). After a short distance you pass the **Redriff Road Bridge** ⓬ on the right, one of a number of old Scherzer bascule bridges – lift bridges that rock or roll back to allow ships to pass – that remain in Surrey Quays but are no longer in use. Continue as far as Cunard Walk then turn left to head east along Greenland Quay, along the dock's southern perimeter, past the **Surrey Docks Watersports Centre** ⓭, to Swedish Quay.

At the end of Swedish Quay turn left to cross over the entrance to **South Dock Marina** ⓮ on Rope Street and go left again to Rainbow Quay. Turn left once more onto South Sea Street, and a short way along on the right is the **Swing Footbridge** ⓯ (moved from South Dock), beyond which is the old entrance lock designed by Sir John Wolfe Barry in 1904, both preserved

Greenland Dock

Food & Drink

1 Brunel Museum Café Gallery: Homemade cakes, excellent coffee and regular exhibitions of local artists' work in the Café Gallery (10am-5pm, £).

18 The Moby Dick: Enjoy home-cooked food with alfresco seating at the water's edge (Mon-Sat 11am-11pm, Sun noon-10.30pm, £).

23 The Blacksmith's Arms: A Fuller's pub with a nice patio garden and good food (noon-midnight, £).

26 The Salt Quay: Imposing Greene King gastropub offering British fare, including Sunday roasts (Mon-Thu 11.30am-11pm, Fri 11.30-midnight, Sat 11am-midnight, Sun 11am-10.30pm, £).

Greenland Dock

Greenland Dock (22½ acres/9ha) is the oldest of London's riverside wet docks. Constructed in 1696 as the Howland Great Wet Doc, it's still largely intact, although all but one of its former entrances and exits have been in-filled or blocked. From the 1720s it was the main dock for Greenland whalers and was renamed Greenland Dock. It still has a working connection to South Dock (now London's largest marina), plus a small marina of its own at the eastern end.

Curlicue 16, a stainless steel decorative curl or twist reminiscent of the anchors scattered along the Thames.

Norway Dock

Return to South Sea Street and turn left on Finland Street, heading east until you reach a narrow channel, just after Norway Gate, which leads to Plover Way. The small body of water on the left (behind the house) is **Norway Dock 17**, most of which was re-excavated to form a water feature for the surrounding residential developments. If you're wondering about the Scandi theme in street names, Rotherhithe has strong links with Scandinavia and is still home to a thriving Scandinavian community. Back on Finland Street, it's just 100m further along to **The Moby Dick 18**, a spacious

but no longer in use. Opposite the lock on Princess Court next to Tide Gauge House is a hydraulic capstan, which was used to calculate the Thames tides that enabled ships to make the tight turn into the lock. Just past the swing bridge, take a detour right along Queen of Denmark Court to see William Pye's 1988 sculpture,

pub overlooking Greenland Dock. Return to walk up Norway Gate and turn right onto the footpath opposite Plover Way to Bonding Yard Walk; keep walking north and at the end, just before Salter Street, the path turns right to join the eastern extremity of Rotherhithe Street. Follow the road around the eastern edge of the park, at the top of which it swings right past **Surrey Docks Farm** ⑲ (see box).

Surrey Docks Farm

A beautiful slice of rural life in the heart of what was one of London's most commercialised districts, Surrey Docks Farm (free, 10am-4pm) is a community farm that aims to educate people about where their food comes. The farm is home to all the usual animals, as well as fruit and vegetable gardens, a farm shop selling fresh produce, meat and eggs, and a café. (See surreydocksfarm.org.uk for information.)

From the farm take the Thames Path that runs along its eastern edge and follow it north past **Durand's Wharf** ⑳ – a peaceful riverside park built on the remains of a 19th-century wharf – to the end, where it leads back to Rotherhithe Road opposite Pearson's Park and close to **Columbia Wharf** ㉑. Columbia Wharf (1864-1976) was the first grain silo in a British port, and has been redeveloped for housing and a hotel, although the wharf's façade has been retained. Nearby **Nelson Dock Pier** ㉒ offers a regular ferry shuttle service to Canary Wharf across the Thames. There are plans to build a pedestrian/cycle bridge – presently called the Brunel Bridge – from Rotherhithe to Canary Wharf, and the proposed routes include Durand's Wharf and Nelson Dock Pier.

From Pearson's Park continue north on Rotherhithe Street, where after around 100m you come to the timber-framed **Blacksmiths Arms** ㉓. Just past the pub take the Thames Path once again, which takes in Pageant Crescent before arriving at a footbridge over a pond that's part of the **Lavender Pond Nature Reserve** ㉔ (see box opposite). Turn left and walk south along the western edge of the pond to Salter Road; then turn right and after a few hundred metres, just past **St Paul's Sports Ground** ㉕, take the footpath on the right to Beatson Walk.

At the end of Beatson Walk you're back on Rotherhithe Street, where you go left and then first right after the Globe Wharf development back to the Thames Path. Follow the path as it wends its way along the Thames, lined with row upon row of apartment blocks, before arriving at the Surrey Water inlet, where you pass the imposing **Salt Quay** ㉖, a pub in a converted warehouse. From the pub go right over the **Bascule Bridge** ❹ – which you encountered earlier – and continue

Salt Quay

Swan Road Mosaic Mural

along Rotherhithe Street and take the fifth turn on the left on Swan Road. Around two-thirds of the way along, at the junction with Kenning Street and on the end of Winchelsea House, is the beautiful **Swan Road Mosaic Mural 27** by David John (1992), depicting a mute swan taking flight. At the end of Swan Road turn right, just past **The Brunel 28** pub, on Brunel Road and 100m along on the right is Rotherhithe railway station from where you started the walk.

Lavender Pond

The northern end of the former Surrey Commercial Docks, Lavender Pond was part of a much larger pond where timber was floated to prevent it drying and cracking. The entrance to the pond was blocked in 1928 when the Port of London Authority built a pumphouse to control water levels in Surrey Docks. The docks closed in 1970 and the pond was in-filled in 1981, but a smaller pond was recreated as part of the reserve, which also includes wet meadows and woodland areas.

Lavender Pond

1 Woolwich Market

2 Royal Arsenal Gatehouse

3 Royal Arsenal Riverside

4 Verbruggen's House

5 Main Guard House

6 Nike

7 Dial Arch

8 Boulangerie Jade

9 Royal Arsenal Farmers' Market

10 Academy Performing Arts

11 Greenwich Heritage Centre

Places of Interest   Food & Drink

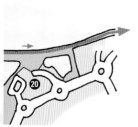

12 Old Laboratory Office
13 Woolwich Arsenal Pier
14 Iron Pier
15 Broadwater Canal
16 Gallions Lake
17 HMP Belmarsh
18 Gallions Hill
19 Tripcock Ness
20 Clocktower
21 Crossness Lighthouse
22 Crossness Pumping Station
23 Crossness Nature Reserve
24 Morgan Belvedere

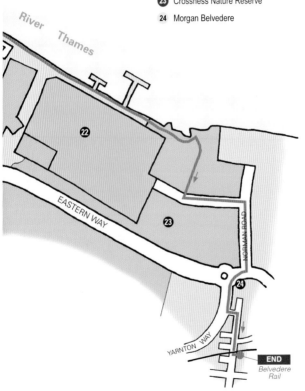

River Thames

EASTERN WAY

NORMAN ROAD

YARNTON WAY

END
Belvedere
Rail

WALK 17

Thamesmead

Distance: 6 miles (9½ km)
Terrain: easy
Duration: 3 hours
Start: Woolwich DLR
End: Belvedere rail
Postcode: SE18 6EU

THAMESMEAD

Once dubbed the 'town of the 21st century', Thamesmead largely consists of a vast sprawling nondescript housing estate, with some peripheral industry, situated on former marshland between Woolwich and Erith (Bexley). The area was developed for housing between the mid-'60s and '80s, but facilities remain woefully inadequate, with relatively few shops and leisure facilities and poor communications – Thamesmead has no tube, DLR or railway stations. Not surprisingly, along with its remoteness and bleak ambience, Thamesmead hasn't proved a popular place to live and has high levels of economic and social deprivation. But it also has some glorious open spaces.

The River Thames here makes its most northerly excursion within Greater London, with 3 miles (5km) of riverbank, around 4½ miles (7k) of canals and six major lakes. There are some 30,000 trees and over 350 acres (142ha) of open space, much of it relatively unspoilt, where wild flowers, woodland and wildlife flourish.

The walk commences in Woolwich town centre (see Walk 21) and heads to the Thames, via historic Woolwich Royal Arsenal, where you follow the Thames Path northeast past Thamesmead West to Gallions Park. From the park the path continues around Tripcock Point and past Thamesmead town centre before arriving at the splendid Crossness Pumping Station, after which we head south, via Crossness Nature Reserve, to finish at Belvedere railway station.

Royal Arsenal Riverside

Start Walking...

Leave Woolwich Arsenal DLR station and cross Woolwich New Road to enter Beresford Square, the venue for **Woolwich Market ❶**. This council-run street market, which has its origins in the 17th century, sells the usual clothes, produce and household goods through the week, while on some Sundays it has a more arts and crafts theme (Mon-Wed 9am-4pm, Thu 9am-1pm, Fri-Sat 9am-4.30pm, Sun 10am-4.30pm – see woolwichmarket.com).

Verbruggen's House

Head north across the square, past the imposing **Royal Arsenal Gatehouse ❷** on your right, and cross over Beresford Street at the traffic lights to enter the **Royal Arsenal Riverside ❸** development, built on the sprawling former Royal Arsenal site (see box). As you walk up No 1 Street, on the right is **Verbruggen's House ❹**, built for Dutch master gun-founder Jan Verbruggen (1712-1781) in 1771. Several early 18th-century buildings – including some attributed to architects Sir John Vanbrugh and Nicholas Hawksmoor – have been retained and incorporated into the new

Royal Arsenal

The forerunner of the Royal Arsenal was established as the Ordnance Storage Depot in 1671 on a 31-acre (12.5ha) site. Called the Warren after the land it was built on – used for breeding rabbits for the pot – it was a facility for the manufacture of armaments such as explosives, fuses and shot, as well as ammunition proofing and explosives research, for the British armed forces. In 1805, at the suggestion of George III, the entire complex became known as the Royal Arsenal and the largest munitions producer in the country. At its peak during the First World War the site extended to 1,285 acres (520ha) and employed around 100,000 people; it also contained almost 150 miles (241km) of railway lines within just 2mi^2 (5.2km^2), the densest railway network in history.

development, including the Royal Brass Foundry, Dial Arch and the Royal Military Academy.

As you enter Royal Arsenal Riverside, on the left is the old **Main Guard House ❺** dating from 1787-8, in front of which is a 10ft (3m) bronze statue of the Greek goddess of victory **Nike ❻** by Greek artist Pavlos Angelos Kougioumtzis. A little further along on the right is the **Dial Arch ❼** gastropub, occupying the former gatehouse (1720) of the Woolwich Arsenal munitions factory. If it's a coffee you crave, there's a branch of **Boulangerie Jade ❽** around the corner in Major Draper Street. It

145

Royal Arsenal Gatehouse

Old Royal Military Academy Building

occupies an old warehouse and retains much of the building's original character. Back on No 1 Street, on the left is Artillery Square (opposite Duke of Wellington Avenue), the venue for the **Royal Arsenal Farmers' Market** (9) (Sat 10am-3pm). At the western end of the Square is the **Academy Performing Arts** (10), based in the former Royal Military Academy building.

To the north of the square is the **Greenwich Heritage Centre** (11), a museum and local history resource centre, while to the east, across No 1 Street, is the **Old Laboratory Office** (12), which controlled the manufacture of ammunition; it used to house the Royal Artillery Museum, Firepower (closed in 2016). At the end of No 1 Street is **Woolwich Arsenal Pier** (13), flanked by

---

Broadwater Canal

Originally called the Pilkington Canal, after its designer Lieutenant Colonel Pilkington, this waterway was built in 1812-16 by convicts to transport materials from the Thames to Woolwich Royal Arsenal, and also to create a defensive boundary to the east. In 1931 the canal was cut back to the junction of the two arms and the whole canal closed in the early '60s. Much of it has been in-filled but part remains as a water feature, now called the Broadwater Canal.

---

two octagonal guardhouses, from where Thames Clippers operate a peak-hour ferry service west along the Thames (see thamesclippers.com).

Leaving the pier head east along the Thames Path, where you pass a plethora of new apartment buildings. A short way along are the remains of the old **Iron Pier** (14), built in 1870. Some 500m further on the path crosses over the **Broadwater Canal** (15) (see box) in Thamesmead West.

Gallions Lake

Just to the east of the canal is freshwater **Gallions Lake** (16), a popular fishing spot. Gallions Reach is a stretch of the Thames between Woolwich and Thamesmead, and lends its name to various locations on both sides of the river (including a DLR station and shopping park in Newham on the north side of the Thames). The name comes from Galyons, a 14th-century family who owned property along this stretch of the river. Just inland from the Thamesmead West estate, across Western Way and adjacent to Woolwich Crown Court, is the notorious **HMP Belmarsh** (17), a high security prison that's often used to detain prisoners for terrorism related offences.

Continuing along the Thames Path, after another 500m or so you pass the ruins of an old wooden slipway and The Potters House Church. Just

Princess Alice Disaster

In 1878, the Tripcock Ness area saw Britain's worst-ever peacetime disaster when the pleasure cruiser *Princess Alice* sank after colliding with the *Bywell Castle*, a huge coal steamer. The *Princess Alice* – crammed with some 900 people returning back up the Thames after a day trip to Sheerness in Kent – sank within minutes in an area of the river where a large amount of raw sewage had been released. As many as 700 of those on board were drowned; some 650 bodies were recovered, but it's estimated that many more were swept out to sea or died later from swallowing the toxic river water.

beyond it is Gallions Park, where a detour into the park reveals **Gallions Hill** 18 ; constructed from rubble and soil excavated during construction of a nearby housing estate, it offers panoramic views across the Thames to Canary Wharf and the City of London.

From here, the Thames Path becomes pleasantly rural; the land is relatively untouched, and wild flowers and woodland left to flourish, along with the wildlife. (This area was the proposed location for the Thames Gateway Bridge across the Thames, which was cancelled in 2008.) After some 600m you arrive at **Tripcock Ness** 19 , aka Tripcock Point,

marked by a signpost, information board and a navigation light beacon. From the late 18th century until the mid-19th century this stretch of the river was home to numerous abandoned ships that were used to house thousands of convicts who were put to work in the Arsenal during the day. On the opposite bank you can see the Barking Creek Barrier, which protects the River Roding from flooding.

Around 500m further on you arrive at Thamesmead's nondescript town centre, which features a retail park centred

Food & Drink

7 **Dial Arch:** A Young's gastropub, offering a British seasonal menu with all the usual pub favourites, plus Sunday roast (Mon-Thu, Sun 10am-11pm, Fri-Sat 10am-11.30pm, £).

8 **Boulangerie Jade:** Just around the corner from Dial Arch, this French artisan bakery and patisserie serves a huge range of cakes and pastries, sandwiches and savouries (Mon-Fri 7am-6pm, Sat 8am-6pm, Sun 8.30am-5pm, £).

24 **Morgan Belvedere:** Classic pub grub including a daily carvery (Mon-Fri 11am-11pm, Sat 9am-11pm, Sun 9am-10.30pm, £).

Tripcock Ness light beacon

Clocktower

around a Morrisons supermarket, a lake and a 19th-century **Clocktower** ⓴ that once stood in Deptford Dockyard (installed here in 1986). There isn't much in the way of eateries, but Morrisons has a café and there's the Cutty Sark pub on Joyce Dawson Way.

Head east along the river and around a kilometre further along you pass the **Crossness Lighthouse** ㉑, installed in 1895 to mark a bend in the river; it's now operated by electricity, with a range of 8 nautical miles. A brief detour inland takes you to the Thamesmead Ecology Study Area.

> ### Crossness Pumping Station
>
> Built by Bazalgette and architect Charles Henry Driver (1832-1900), the Grade I listed Crossness Pumping Station was officially opened by the Prince of Wales in April 1865. The Beam Engine House was constructed in the Romanesque (Norman) style in gault (clay) brick, with considerable ornamentation, red brick arches and dog-tooth string courses. However, the interior is its real tour de force; featuring spectacular colourful and ornate Victorian wrought and cast ironwork, it was described as 'a masterpiece of engineering – a Victorian cathedral of ironwork' by architectural expert Nikolaus Pevsner. It contains the four original pumping engines, among the largest remaining rotative beam engines in the world with 52-ton flywheels and 47-ton beams. Although modern diesel engines were subsequently introduced, the old beam engines remained in service until work on a new sewerage treatment plant began in 1956. (For more information and open days, see crossness.org.uk.)

(see box), a masterpiece of Victorian engineering. In the early 19th century, London's water supply and the Thames were heavily polluted with sewage, and

Beyond the lighthouse the river curves and there's a brief respite from housing estates, before you reach the magnificent **Crossness Pumping Station** ㉒

Crossness Pumping Station (all 3)

Crossness Nature Reserve

resulting cholera outbreaks killed up to 20,000 people annually. However, it was the 'Great Stink' of 1858, when the Houses of Parliament became so smelly that members demanded action, that was the catalyst for the creation of the sewer system London still has today. It was created by Sir Joseph William Bazalgette (1819-1891), who built 83 miles (134km) of 'interceptory' sewers that prevented raw sewage from running into the Thames and took it to the east of London; there it was pumped into the river with minimal effect on the population via four major pumping stations, one of which was Crossness.

Just beyond the pumping station and sewage treatment works – where you may wish to walk more swiftly! – the Thames Path crosses the top of the **Crossness Nature Reserve** ㉓; it's just across the Thames from the vast Ford Dagenham engine plant on the north bank, which employed some 40,000 workers in the post-war years. The reserve (63 acres/25.5ha) incorporates some of the last remaining grazing marshes in Greater London, part of the original Thames floodplain named the Erith Marshes. Its wetlands are perfect for wildlife, particularly birds, and more than 130 species have been recorded

here, including little egret, sanderling, ringed ouzel, Cetti's warbler and Dartford warbler. A deep-water lagoon attracts wintering visitors such as teal, wigeon, gadwall and shoveler, and winter flooding brings lapwing, dunlin, redshank and gulls. Viewing facilities include a bird hide, sand martin wall, bat cave, artificial nesting cliff, and a boardwalk around a reedbed frequented by water rail, sedge warblers, willow warblers and reed buntings.

Leave the Thames Path just after the sewage treatment works (before the Riverside Resource energy recovery plant – a huge white building with a green stripe) on the track to the right (signposted Belvedere Station) and turn left on the path that crosses the nature reserve to Norman Road. At the bottom of Norman Road, cross over the Picardy Manorway (A2016) and turn right and follow the path on the left to Clydesdale Way. This passes the **Morgan Belvedere** ㉔ , a sprawling modern pub with alfresco seating that's an excellent venue for lunch or, if you prefer, coffee and cake. From the pub it's just a short walk south on Clydesdale Way and then Norman Road, which leads to Belvedere railway station – and the end of the walk.

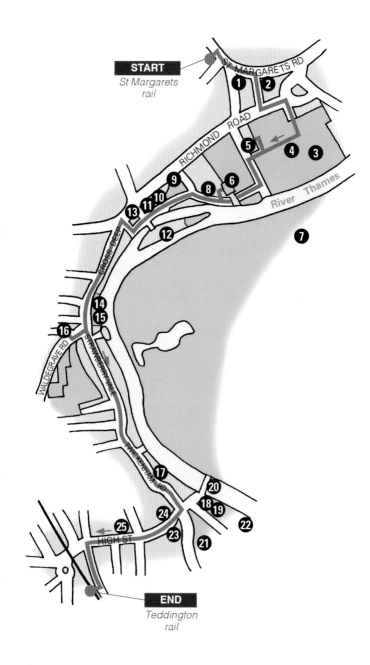

● Places of Interest   ○ Food & Drink

WALK 18

Twickenham to Teddington

Distance: 4 miles (6½ km)

Terrain: easy

Duration: 2-3 hours

Start: St Margarets rail

End: Teddington rail

Postcode: TW1 2LH

Twickenham is an affluent district in the borough of Richmond-upon-Thames, in southwest London, bordering the River Thames. The area was first mentioned as *Tuican hom* or *Tuiccanham* in an 8th-century charter that ceded the area to Waldhere, Bishop of London. In Norman times it was part of the manor of Isleworth, mentioned in the *Domesday Book* of 1086. The area was mainly farmland during the Middle Ages, while the river provided opportunities for fishing, boatbuilding and trade. In the 18th century it was the site of the Great Vitriol Works, which produced sulphuric acid, and the country's first industrial gunpowder factory. The historic riverside area is noted for its splendid 18th-century mansions, many of which survive intact, including Marble Hill, Strawberry Hill and York House.

Today, Twickenham is best known as the home of English rugby union (at Twickenham Stadium), but the town has much more to offer, including a number of excellent (riverside) pubs, restaurants and cafés, comprehensive rail links, attractive housing, good schools, an abundance of green areas and, of course, the river.

South of Twickenham is Teddington – the name comes from an Old English tribal leader, Tuda – known in Saxon and Norman times as *Todyngton* and *Tutington*. Today, it's a peaceful residential area, with many of the same attributes as Twickenham and close proximity to expansive Bushy Park to the south and lovely Ham across the river.

The walk starts in St Margarets – one of London's first garden suburbs – in East Twickenham and goes south via Marble Hill Park and along the Thames to York House Gardens and Strawberry Hill House. We then continue south to Teddington to finish our walk.

River Thames, Twickenham

Start Walking…

Exit St Margarets railway station and go right on St Margarets Road past **St Margarets ❶**, a pleasant gastropub with a nice garden. Continue for another 200m and turn right down Sandycoombe Road, where **Sandycombe Lodge ❷**, former home of painter J.M.W. Turner (1775-1851), is on the left. In 1807, Turner purchased a plot of land and built the handsome Regency villa you see today to his own design, with advice from his friend Sir John Soane, the leading architect of the day. In 2010 the house was bequeathed to the nation along with a collection of material about the artist and has been restored to its former glory (see turnershouse.org for opening times and prices).

Continue along Sandycoombe Road to the end, go left on Richmond Road and cross over to enter **Marble Hill Park ❸** (see box). Follow the path around to the left to the car park then take the path south and turn right after around 200m to see **Marble Hill House ❹** (entry fee). A few hundred metres past the house is **The Coach House Café 5** , a good place for morning coffee. From here a path leads west to Orleans Road, where you turn left and follow the road down the side of the park until it swings right into Riverside, with Orleans Gardens on your left and the Thames just beyond.

Marble Hill Park & House

Marble Hill Park (66 acres/27ha) surrounds Marble Hill House, a beautiful Palladian villa on the north bank of the Thames. It's the last complete survivor of the many handsome villas and gardens that bordered the river between Richmond and Hampton Court in the 18th century. Designed by Roger Morris and built between 1724 and 1729 for Henrietta Howard – Countess of Suffolk and mistress of George II (when he was Prince of Wales) – the house is now managed by English Heritage. Its grand interiors have been beautifully restored and conjure up the atmosphere of fashionable Georgian life, with a collection of early Georgian furniture and some fine paintings, as well as a splendid collection of Chinoiserie (the Lazenby Bequest). The house is open weekends for guided tours, but the park is free to enter. It was laid out in the early 18th century – with advice from Alexander Pope and Charles Bridgeman – with terraced lawns, avenues of chestnuts and scattered trees. (For more information see english-heritage.org.uk/visit/places/marble-hill-house.)

Orleans House

Just past Orleans Gardens go right to visit **Orleans House Gallery ❻** (free, Tue-Sun 10am-5pm, orleanshousegallery.org), one of Greater London's finest small galleries. Opened in 1972, it houses the art collection of the London borough of Richmond-upon-Thames, one of the most outstanding fine art collections in London, comprising some 3,200 paintings, drawings, photographs, prints and objects dating from the early 18th century to the present day. The original house was built in 1710 for James Johnston (1655-1737), Joint Secretary of State for Scotland. However, it takes its name from Louis-Phillippe, Duc D'Orleans (later King of France), who lived there between 1813 and 1815. Most of the house was demolished in the '20s but the elegant Octagonal Room remains. There's a café in the old stables at the start of Riverside, and close by is Hammertons Ferry (daily March to early October, weekends only Dec-Feb weather permitting – see hammertonsferry.com), from where you can get a boat across the Thames to visit **Ham House & Garden** ❼ .

The White Swan

From the gallery return to Riverside, where after around 100m you come to **The White Swan** ❽ , a traditional 17th-century pub with a lovely riverside terrace. A short way past the pub on the right is Sion Road, which contains an attractive 18th-century terrace with unusual Egyptian-style decoration under the eaves. Back on Riverside you cut through the middle of

York House Gardens

York House Gardens (free, 7.30am-dusk, 9am Sundays, accessed via Sion Road and the Riverside footpath) were commissioned by Sir Ratan Tata (1871-1918), a Parsee industrialist from Mumbai who purchased York House in 1906. Tata, whose family still runs one of the largest companies in India, installed a group of striking Italian Carrara marble statues (Grade II listed) in the gardens, consisting of naked females representing the Oceanides (sea nymphs) of Greek mythology. These include two winged horses with a female charioteer in a shell chariot, plunging through the water at the top of a cascade and pool, while seven other figures sit on or clamber up rocks. Some of the 'naked ladies' are posed in unusual attitudes and can come as a surprise to the unsuspecting visitor!

beautiful **York House Gardens** ❾ (see box) – the two sides are divided by the road but connected by a handsome stone footbridge. Over to the right is York House (Grade II listed), a fine 17th-century building and now the HQ of the London borough of Richmond.

At the end of Riverside turn right into Church Lane to see **St Mary's Parish Church** ❿ , aka St Mary the Virgin, an 18th-century church incorporating an

St Mary's Parish Church

settlements in the area (free, Tue and Sat 11am-3pm, Sun 2-4pm, twickenham-museum.org.uk).

Eel Pie Island

Food & Drink

⑤ The Coach House Café: An excellent café in a peaceful setting in Marble Hill Park, serving tasty home cooking and delicious cakes (10am-5pm, £).

⑧ The White Swan: Fireplaces, stripped floors and excellent food in a glorious location, with one of the best beer gardens in London (Tue-Sat 11am-11pm, Sun-Mon 11am-10.30pm, £).

⑲ The Anglers: Family-friendly Fuller's pub with a menu of fish specials, a large garden and a kids' play area (11am-11pm, £-££).

Return to the river for a view of **Eel Pie Island ⑫** – the name comes from pies that were served on the island in the 19th century – a 9-acre (3.6ha) eyot or ait in the Thames. It was the site of Eel Pie Island Hotel, a genteel 19th-century hostelry that hosted ballroom dancing in the '20s and '30s, and later featured major rock and R&B bands in the '60s (the hotel burned down in 1971). You can reach the island via a footbridge a short way along The Embankment.

Continue south, and after you pass **Diamond Jubilee Gardens ⑬** (Mon-Fri 9am-5pm, weekends vary), follow the road round to the right, away from the river (there's no Thames Path here), to Wharf Lane. Walk to the top and turn left onto King Street and again to Cross Deep. Continue south to **Radnor Gardens ⑭** – named for the 4th Earl of Radnor – a small public riverside garden with a bowling green, children's playground, café and Mortimer Brown's **Twickenham War Memorial ⑮**.

Twickenham War Memorial

earlier 15th-century tower. After the nave of the previous church collapsed in 1713, it was reconstructed in Neo-Classical style by John James. It's the burial place of poet Alexander Pope (1688-1744), who lived in Twickenham from 1719 until his death. Opposite the church on Church Lane is **Twickenham Museum ⑪**, opened in 1860, although the current museum – housed in a Georgian building (ca. 1720, Grade II listed) – dates from 2001. The museum's permanent exhibition records and celebrates the history, life and growth of the various

The First World War memorial features a bronze figure of a soldier – clearly victorious, smiling and waving his hat in the air – with three bronze panels of low relief sculpture and a coat of arms on a stone plinth. Just past the gardens go right on Waldegrave Road, where **Strawberry Hill House** ⑯ (entry fee, see box) is a short way along on the left.

Teddington Lock footbridge

From Strawberry Hill retrace your steps to Cross Deep and go right on Strawberry Vale (adjacent to the river), which leads into Twickenham Road and then Manor Road. Just before Manor Road Recreation Ground you pass the **RNLI Teddington Lifeboat Station** ⑰, one of the first to cover a river rather than estuarial waters or the sea. At the end of Manor Road turn left on Ferry Road and head back towards the river. On the right is **Tide End Cottage** ⑱, a pretty traditional Greene King pub tucked away in a terrace of houses; behind it on Broom Road is **The Anglers** ⑲, a popular riverside pub with a large terrace.

Its garden overlooks **Teddington Lock** ⑳, the largest lock complex on the Thames with three locks – which separates the tidal from the non-tidal river – and two

Strawberry Hill House

A Gothic castle of undoubted charm and originality, visiting Strawberry Hill is something of a theatrical experience. Built in 1698, it was originally a modest house, but from 1747 was transformed by Horace Walpole (1717-1797) – the son of Britain's first Prime Minister, Robert Walpole – into Britain's finest example of Georgian Gothic architecture and interior design. Walpole was a dedicated collector, and Strawberry Hill was expanded to house his huge assortment of 'treasures'. Whereas nearby houses such as Marble Hill (see page 153) were based on classical traditions, Walpole used the architecture of Gothic cathedrals as his inspiration, adding battlements and towers as he saw fit; the project evolved in the way medieval cathedrals did, over time and with no fixed overall design. The exterior resembles a wedding cake, while inside the gloomy hall and staircase provide a dramatic contrast to magnificent rooms bedecked in gold and crimson. Now restored to its original 1790s splendour, the house has been open to visitors for over 250 years, although Walpole only allowed four visitors a day (and no children!). The house is complemented by a romantic garden inspired by William Kent and the English Landscape Movement. (For information, see strawberryhillhouse.org.uk.)

footbridges across the river (to Ham). A bit further along Broom Road is the sports ground of **St Mary's University** ㉑, a research university founded in 1850, and the oldest Catholic university in the UK. Opposite is **The Lensbury Club** ㉒, a 4-star hotel set within 25 acres (10ha) of landscaped grounds.

Return to Ferry Road and turn left, where just past the junction with Kingston Road is the **Landmark Arts Centre** ㉓, housed in

Landmark Arts Centre

the former St Alban's Church (Grade II* listed), dedicated to Saint Alban, the first English martyr. The Landmark is a charity offering a diverse programme of arts events, fairs and classes, concerts and exhibitions. Behind the church are Udney Hall Gardens, a remnant of the grounds of Udney Hall, former home of Sir Charles Duncombe (1648-1711), Lord Mayor of London. Opposite the Landmark is **St Mary with St Alban Church 24** (Grade II* listed), the oldest parts of which date from the 16th century.

Ferry Road leads to Teddington High Street, where there's a wealth of food and drink options, including a few decent pubs; our favourite is **The King's Head 25** some 100m along on the right, a renovated Victorian gastropub with snugs, log fires and a walled garden. From here, continue along the High Street and turn left on Station Road which leads to Teddington railway station – and the end of the walk.

Strawberry Hill House

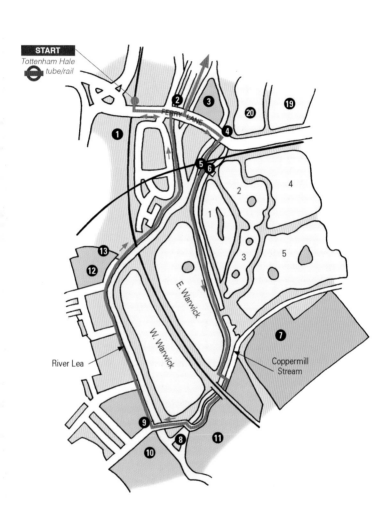

START

Tottenham Hale
tube/rail

FERRY LANE

River Lea

E. Warwick

W. Warwick

Coppermill
Stream

Places of Interest   Food & Drink

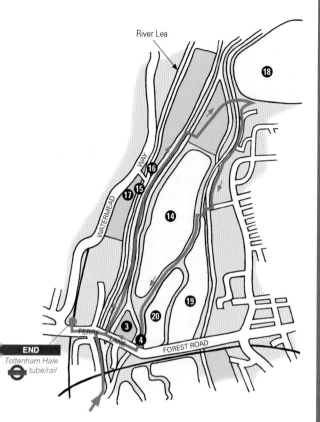

1. Tottenham Hale Retail Park
2. Tottenham Lock
3. Paddock Community Nature Park
4. Ferry Boat Inn
5. Walthamstow Wetlands Visitor Centre
6. Engine House Café
7. Coppermill
8. Lee Valley Marina Springfield
9. Riverside Café
10. Springfield Park
11. Walthamstow Marshes
12. Markfield Park
13. Markfield Beam Engine & Museum
14. Lockwood Reservoir
15. Stonebridge Lock
16. Stonebridge Lock Waterside Café
17. Tottenham Marshes
18. Banbury Reservoir
19. High Maynard Reservoir
20. Low Maynard Reservoir

Walthamstow Wetlands

Distance: 6 miles (10 km)

Terrain: easy

Duration: 3 hours

Start/End: Tottenham Hale tube/rail

Postcode: N17 9LR

WALTHAMSTOW WETLANDS

The beautiful Walthamstow Wetlands are one of the largest urban wetland nature reserves in Europe, part of the Lea (referring to the River Lea or Lee) Valley Special Protection Area and home to many important wildlife species, particularly migrating waterfowl. The Wetlands – which encompass ten reservoirs providing water to 3½ million homes – were closed to the general public for 150 years. Open to everyone since October 2017 (access is free), the Wetlands cover 521 acres (211ha) of land and water, including 13 miles (21km) of footpaths and cycle track – some of which are closed periodically to protect nesting birds or special wildlife habitats – and eight islands. The well-stocked reservoirs are a popular fishing spot and the largest recreational fishery in London. Note that dogs aren't allowed in the Wetlands.

Walthamstow Wetlands has been designated a Site of Special Scientific Interest (SSSI) due to the reservoirs' importance to breeding, migratory and wintering water birds. Waterfowl such as pochard, gadwall and shoveler overwinter here, and it's a stopover for migrating sandpipers, redshank, lapwings and many more. The 'common' kingfisher breeds here, as does the grey heron (there's a famous heronry on the wooded islands of Reservoir No 1), tufted duck, little egret, cormorant, bittern and other waterfowl. You're also likely to see soaring buzzards, peregrine falcons, kestrels and other birds of prey, while on warm summer evenings bats emerge from their roosting sites to feed on insects over the water. Furthermore, some 300 species of plant have been recorded in the wooded areas, grass banks, fen and open water habitats of the reservoirs.

The walk commences at Tottenham Hale tube/railway station and continues east past Tottenham Lock and the Paddock Community Nature Park to the Walthamstow Wetlands Visitor Centre. From here we head south to the Coppermill and west to Springfield Park, from where we go north to Markfield Park and follow the path past Tottenham Lock and Tottenham Marshes to Banbury Reservoir, before returning south through the Wetlands to our starting point.

Start Walking...

As you leave Tottenham Hale station, just over the road is **Tottenham Hale Retail Park 1**, your best bet for a coffee boost. From the station, turn left and head east along Ferry Lane. After 150m, the road crosses the Lee Navigation (as the canalised River Lea/Lee is called), providing a view of **Tottenham Lock 2**,

Tottenham Lock

and soon after (on the left) there's a gate to **Paddock Community Nature Park 3** (dawn to dusk). Surrounded on two sides by water, the Paddock provides an important refuge for water birds and other aquatic animals, while its rich array of plant life includes hawthorn, elder, buddleia, wild geraniums, purple flowering comfrey, white daisies and pink dog roses. The wilderness area in the centre of the Paddock has grown naturally to form young woodland and scrub dominated by elder, willow and blackberry, providing a valuable habitat for a wide range of wildlife.

Just past the Paddock you cross over the River Lea (see box) and arrive at your first potential watering hole, the **Ferry Boat Inn 4**. Just over the road from the pub is the entrance to Walthamstow Wetlands. Walk along the river and through the car park (fee) to reach the **Walthamstow Wetlands**

River Lea

The River Lea (also spelt 'Lee') originates in Leagrove near Luton in the Chiltern Hills and flows generally southeast through East London, before joining the Bow Creek tidal estuary and the River Thames. It's one of one of the largest rivers in London and the easternmost major tributary of the Thames. Much of the river has been canalised to provide a navigable route for boats, known as the Lee Navigation. The upper reaches of the Lea have been a major source of drinking water for London since 1613, when an artificial waterway – the New River – was constructed. The river features prominently in the Walthamstow Wetlands, running along both sides of the reservoirs.

Visitor Centre 5 (9.30am-4/5pm, walthamstowwetlands.com) and **Engine House Café 6**. Both are located in the spectacular, brick-built Marine Engine

Walthamstow Wetlands

Engine House

2 miles (3.2km), merging with the Lee Navigation opposite Springfield Park. At the end of the reservoirs the stream flows southwest, parallel with Coppermill Lane, where the **Coppermill** **7** (see box opposite) and the Coppermill Water Treatment Works are a few hundred metres off to the left.

House, originally the Ferry Lane Pumping Station, constructed in 1894 and now converted to service visitors. The Victorian chimney has been rebuilt as bijou accommodation for winged visitors, where some 50 small openings on its flanks provide perfect nesting sites for swifts, while slits on its south side are home to the site's large bat population. Meanwhile, from the centre's viewing platform you can survey the pretty Coppermill Stream and six of the 19th-century reservoirs (see box), which today appear to be natural lakes with their organic shapes and wooded banks.

From the Engine House take the path south to the right of the Coppermill Stream (named after the Coppermill), between Reservoir No 1 and Warwick Reservoir East. The stream is a minor tributary of the River Lea that rises close to the Lockwood Reservoir and flows south for

Walthamstow Reservoirs

The Wetlands consists of ten reservoirs, which cover an area of 316 acres (125ha), managed by Thames Water. They were constructed (quite literally dug by hand!) on marshland between 1853 and 1904, a project undertaken by the East London Waterworks Company (ELWC). This was one of eight private water companies that were absorbed by the Metropolitan Water Board in 1904; this, in turn, was abolished in 1974, when control was transferred to the Thames Water Authority (now Thames Water).

Continue along Coppermill Lane, passing another entrance to the reserve, and cross over the Coppermill Stream just before the **Lee Valley Marina Springfield** **8**, a river marina with some 200

Lea Valley Marina Springfield

moorings for narrowboats and pleasure craft. Follow the path around to the west and cross the River Lea over the bridge to Spring Hill, where you find the **Riverside Café** ❾. There are two parks here: the Lee Valley Springhill Sports Ground to the north and **Springfield Park** ❿ (dawn to dusk) to the south. Delightfully situated alongside the River Lea, 38-acre (15ha) Springfield Park opened in 1905 and was created from the grounds of three private houses, one of which, the White House,

Walthamstow Marshes

is now the park's café. Features include a pond with an island and lawns scattered with trees, offering spectacular views over **Walthamstow Marshes** ⓫. Just south

Food & Drink

❹ **Ferry Boat Inn:** Celebrated 18th-century pub with a beer garden serving classic pub grub and real ales (Sun-Wed 11am-11pm, Thu-Sat 11am-midnight, £).

❻ **Engine House Café:** Café in the restored Engine House at Walthamstow Wetlands – perfect for morning coffee or lunch (9.30am-4/5pm, £).

⓰ **Stonebridge Lock Waterside Café:** A nice spot for a drink or snack alongside Tottenham Marshes (Tue-Fri 8am-5pm, Sat-Sun 8am-6pm, closed Mon, £).

Coppermill

There has been a mill on the site since at least 1086 – when it was listed in the *Domesday Book* – variously used to produce flour, gunpowder, paper, leather and linseed oil. The current mill gets its name from the halfpenny and penny Conder tokens (named after businessman James Conder, 1761-1823) which were struck here during the late 18th and early 19th centuries in response to a shortage of small denomination coins. The Victorian Coppermill was acquired in 1859 by the East London Waterworks Company, who re-purposed the mill as a pumping house to drain the marshes during the construction of the Walthamstow reservoirs. They also added an Italianate tower/loggia (Grade II listed) in 1864 to accommodate a Cornish Bull engine. The iconic tower includes a unique platform providing visitors with panoramic views over the Wetlands and London's skyline to the south.

of the Wetlands, the marshes comprise 91 acres (37ha) of semi-natural wetland; this is where aero-designer Alliott Verdon Roe (1877-1958) made the first British powered flight in his Roe I Triplane in 1909.

Markfield Beam Engine & Museum

The Markfield Beam Engine was the star of the show at Tottenham and Wood Green sewage treatment works and pumping station, opened in 1864. Built between 1886 and 1888 and commissioned on 12th July 1888, the 100-horsepower beam pumping engine is housed in a Victorian engine house (both Grade II listed), which saw continuous service until late 1905, when it was relegated to standby duty for storm water pumping. It ceased operation in 1964 but has been restored to full working order and can be seen operating under steam power on 'steam' days (see mbeam.org for information and opening times).

From the café continue north past the Lea Rowing Club – the river here has been a popular rowing venue since the mid-19th century, when Spring Hill was dubbed the 'Henley of the Lea' – alongside the River Lea and opposite Warwick Reservoir West. Around 500m north is **Markfield Park** 12 , which has an adventure playground, sports pavilion and another popular café (and toilets), although its main claim to fame is the historic **Markfield Beam Engine & Museum** 13 (free entry – see box).

From the museum continue northeast along the river, passing under a railway line and crossing Pymme's Brook where it merges with the Lee Navigation, just before Ferry Lane and **Tottenham Lock** 2 that you passed earlier. The paired lock was originally nearer to Stonebridge, but was relocated to its current location in 1845 when the cut was built, creating a junction just south of the lock. Named after local land owner William Pymme, Pymme's Brook is a minor tributary of the River Lea which rises in Hadley Wood in Enfield. Cross over the lock and continue along the path past a cluster of industrial buildings, with the Lee Navigation on your left and the natural River Lea on your right. A few hundred metres further along you find yourself hemmed in by waterways – a delightful stretch lined with narrowboats and greenery – with the Navigation and Pymme's Brook on your left and the River Lea and **Lockwood Reservoir** 14 on your right.

Around two-thirds of the way along the reservoir you come to paired **Stonebridge Lock** 15 on the Navigation, where you can cross over to **Stonebridge Lock Waterside Café** 16 if you need to refuel. To the west are **Tottenham Marshes** 17 (see box opposite), which cover an area of over 100 acres (40ha) and were the original home of Tottenham Hotspur Football Club in 1882. From the café, cross back over the lock, turn left and continue on the path until you come to the parkland north of Lockwood Reservoir; cut across diagonally to the northeast and

Wood Sandpiper

cross over the River Lea. The path loops southeast past the corner of **Banbury Reservoir** ⑱, the northernmost of the Wetlands' reservoirs. As you approach the houses, turn right and continue south, via Travers Close, alongside the River Lea and Lockwood Reservoir.

After some 300m you arrive at the Lockwood Way entrance to Walthamstow Wetlands, where you cross over the River Lea and the Lee Navigation and follow the path along the edge of the **High Maynard** ⑲ and **Low Maynard Reservoirs** ⑳. The reservoirs are home to a large concentration of breeding waterfowl and in winter the island on High Maynard is a popular roosting place for cormorants, while the fringes are home to a variety of rare plants, such as creeping marshwort and brookweed. Just past the end of Lockwood Reservoir is the **Paddock Community Nature Park** ❸, shortly before the path emerges on to Forest Road alongside the Coppermill Stream. Go right on Forest Road, and a short way along you are back at the **Ferry Boat Inn** ❹, a nice spot to celebrate completing the walk.

From the pub continue west along Ferry Lane to Tottenham Hale tube/railway station from where you started – and the end of the walk.

Tottenham Marshes

One of the last remaining examples of semi-natural wetland in Greater London, the marshes contain a variety of plant communities typical of a former flood plain location, such as a range of neutral grassland types, sedge marsh, reed swamp, sallow scrub and areas of tall herb vegetation. Originally a flood plain of the River Lea, the marshes were later used for recreation, gravel extraction and landfill. In the late 19th century the Wild Marsh East was bisected when the River Lea was diverted to accommodate the construction of some of the Lea Valley Reservoir Chain (which number 13 and include the ten Walthamstow Reservoirs).

Walthamstow Wetlands

START
Tower Hill tube

Wapping Woods

TOWER HILL

EAST SMITH FIELD

WAPPING LANE

23

22
21
20
19
17
18
16
13 14
15

TOWER BRIDGE

River

1

2
3
4
5
6 7
8
12
9 10
11

24

WAPPING HIGH STREET

① Tower of London
② St Katharine Docks
③ White Mulberries
④ Dickens Inn
⑤ Alderman Stairs
⑥ Hermitage Riverside Memorial Garden
⑦ Smith's Wapping
⑧ Wapping Pier Head
⑨ Wapping Old Stairs
⑩ Town of Ramsgate
⑪ Oliver's Wharf
⑫ St John's Churchyard
⑬ Thames River Police Museum

END
Bromley-by-Bow tube

A12

DEVAS STREET

MORRIS ROAD

BURDETT ROAD

34
38

COMMERCIAL RD

EAST INDIA DOCK ROAD

29
33
36 37
30 32
31 35

River Thames

● Places of Interest   Food & Drink

WALK 20

Wapping to Three Mills Island

Distance: 5½ miles (9 km)
Terrain: easy
Duration: 3 hours
Start: Tower Hill tube
End: Bromley-by-Bow tube
Postcode: EC3N 4DJ

WAPPING TO THREE MILLS ISLAND

Wapping is thought to be of Saxon origin, named after a leader called Waeppa, although others claim the name derives from *wapol* (meaning marsh). Its Thameside location meant it had a strong maritime character well into the 20th century, inhabited by sailors, mastmakers, boat-builders, block-makers, instrument-makers, victuallers, dockers and other trades associated with seafaring. The opening of the London Docks in 1805 (see map below) transformed the village of Wapping, and it thrived up until the Second World War, when the area was devastated by German bombing.

The docks were closed in the '60s and Wapping went into severe economic, physical and social decline, although there has been extensive regeneration since the '80s. However, unlike most other regenerated areas of London, Wapping seems immune to gentrification and retains much of its historic character and atmosphere, although it's eerily quiet much of the time. Neighbouring Limehouse shares much of Wapping's history of seafaring, decline and rebirth as a Thameside residential district.

Today, the riverside is a fascinating place to explore, with a blend of modern apartment blocks, converted warehouses and historic houses, seemingly untouched for centuries. The final destination is Three Mills Island in Bromley-by-Bow, a backwater that has changed little over the centuries.

The walk commences at Tower Hill and heads east along the riverside through the historic dockland areas of Wapping, Shadwell and Limehouse. We continue along the Limehouse Cut to Bow Creek and the River Lea, before visiting the House Mill Museum on Three Mills Island and ending in Bromley-by-Bow.

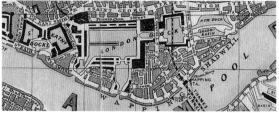

London Docks

Start Walking...

Leaving Tower Hill tube station, go right down the steep steps and through Tower Hill subway, with the **Tower of London** ① directly in front of you. Follow the path to the left, which skirts the moat and keep, through Tower Bridge Approach subway and right past Tower Bridge House to the haven of **St Katharine Docks** ② (see box). Follow the path straight ahead along the top of the marina – lined with cafés and restaurants – and go right past Ivory House, built in 1858 and the only remaining original warehouse, now home to the Medieval Banquet, a theatrical dining experience. Go through the archway and turn left, where a few steps along is **White Mulberries** ③, a cosy café overlooking the marina.

St Katharine Docks

Designed by Thomas Telford and opened in 1828, St Katharine Docks were one of several commercial docks that comprised the Port of London, although their origins can be traced back to the 10th century when King Edgar the Peaceful (943-975) gifted land to 13 knights to use for trade. There's been evidence of a dock here since 1125, and the name comes from the former hospital of St Katharine by the Tower, endowed by Empress Matilda (1102-1167, and briefly Queen of England though never crowned) and built in the 12th century. The docks closed in 1968 and today comprise offices, apartments, a hotel, shops, bars, restaurants, yacht marina and other recreational facilities.

Dickens Inn

From the café, continue along the path east and turn right over the footbridge to Marble Quay, where the KERB street food market is held on Fridays (noon to 2pm) in front of the weather-boarded **Dickens Inn** ④. From the quay go right and then left past the Mala Indian restaurant to Mews Street, where you turn right and then left along St Katharine's Way; from here there are magnificent views of Tower Bridge and Butler's Wharf on the opposite bank of the Thames. After a few steps you pass HMS President, a 'stone frigate' or shore establishment of the Royal Naval Reserve unit (not to be confused with the ship *HMS President*, permanently moored on the Thames near Blackfriars Bridge), and **Alderman Stairs** ⑤, one of many original 'watermen's stairs' down to the Thames.

At the end of the road, go right along historic Wapping High Street. Many of the former warehouses and docks have been demolished and replaced with new apartment blocks or converted into flats, although the survivors provide a nostalgic flavour of what Wapping was

St Katharine Docks

Wapping Old Stairs

like in bygone days. A short way along on the right is the **Hermitage Riverside Memorial Garden** 6 in commemoration of Londoners who lost their lives during the Blitz in the Second World War.

London Docks

Constructed in Wapping between 1799 and 1815, London Docks were the closest docks to the City until St Katharine Docks were built two decades later. The docks occupied around 30 acres (12ha), and consisted of the Western and Eastern Dock, linked by Tobacco Dock. The larger Western Dock was connected to the Thames via Hermitage Basin to the southwest and Wapping Basin to the south, while the smaller Eastern Dock was connected to the Thames via the Shadwell Basin. The docks closed in 1969 and the in-filled land remained largely derelict until the '80s. Today, only Hermitage Basin and Shadwell Basin survive, while the Ornamental Canal runs across the southern part of the Western Dock site from Hermitage Basin to Tobacco Dock and on to Shadwell Basin.

Continue along Wapping High Street, where just past the garden is **Smith's Wapping** 7 , an excellent seafood restaurant. A bit further on, on either side of the street, is **Wapping Pier Head** 8 , two rows of beautiful 18th-century townhouses, separated by gardens. They were built for dock officials – number 3 on the right was the old Customs House – and are now converted into very desirable flats. A few steps further on, tucked between number 11 and a quaint old pub is **Wapping Old Stairs** 9 , another of the many old stairways providing access to the river. Near here was the Execution Dock (see box opposite), set at the low-tide mark in the Thames, which was the limit of the jurisdiction of the British Admiralty. It was the Admiralty's task to deal with crimes at sea, and offenders were executed in London irrespective of where their crimes were committed.

Town of Ramsgate

The pub next to the stairs is the excellent **Town of Ramsgate** 10 , named after the fishermen of Ramsgate in Kent, who landed their catches at Wapping Old Stairs to avoid taxes imposed higher up the river. It's a traditional boozer dating back to the 16th century – although the current pub is Victorian – and is famous for being the place where notorious 'Hanging' Judge Jeffreys was apprehended as he tried to flee Britain disguised as a sailor. Jeffreys (1645-1689) had presided over the Bloody

Food & Drink

③ White Mulberries: Super little café nestling in St Katharine Docks – the perfect place for morning coffee and a pastry (Mon-Fri 7.30am-5pm, Sat 8am-6pm, Sun 8.30am-6pm, £).

⑱ The Turk's Head: A family-run pub and café serving great breakfasts and brunches (Mon-Fri from 8am, weekends from 9am, closes 5pm Sun-Wed and 10/11pm otherwise, £).

㉛ The Narrow: Gordon Ramsey's Limehouse gastropub, offering modern British cuisine (020-7592 7950, Mon-Thu noon-11pm, Fri 7.30am-11pm, Sat 8am-11pm, Sun 8am-10.30pm, ££).

Execution Dock

Used for over 400 years (until around 1830) to execute pirates, smugglers and mutineers, the infamous Execution Dock is thought to have been close to Wapping Old Stairs (the exact site is unknown). The condemned were hanged or gibbeted in the Wapping waters until three tides had passed over their swollen bodies. The notorious Captain Kidd (1654-1701), who was convicted of piracy and murder, was executed here in 1701; his body was gibbeted over the Thames at Tilbury Point for three years as a warning to would-be pirates.

Next door to the pub is **Oliver's Wharf ⑪**, a former tea warehouse built in Gothic style in 1869-70, and one of the first riverside warehouses to be converted into apartments. Opposite is **St John's Churchyard ⑫** where the tower is all that remains of the 18th-century St John the Evangelist church, destroyed in the Second World War. To the right of the churchyard on Scandrett Street is St John's Old School (founded 1695), now private houses. Note the handsome former school building with two stone statues of children in the bluecoat charity school uniform tucked into niches on the second floor.

Assizes after the Duke of Monmouth's unsuccessful rebellion against James II in 1685 and took great pleasure in sending hundreds to their execution. The tables were turned after the Glorious Revolution of 1688, which overthrew James II and replaced him with William & Mary. Reviled by the public, Jeffreys was arrested but escaped the rope, dying of natural causes a year later while incarcerated in the Tower of London.

Oliver's Wharf

Around 200m further along the High Street is the **Thames River Police Museum** 13, housed within the Metropolitan Police's Marine Policing Unit. The Thames River Police was the world's first organised police force, established in 1798, three decades before Robert Peel set up the Metropolitan Police Force, and the museum records its history (viewing by arrangement, see thamespolicemuseum.org.uk). Next door is St John's Wharf and beyond it yet another historic pub, **The Captain Kidd** 14, named after the notorious pirate (see Execution Dock box on page 171).

Turk's Head

16. Walk north through the Rose Gardens to Meeting House Alley. If you're hungry, a detour to the left along Green Bank, past **Wapping Gardens** 17 – created on the site of a slum clearance and opened in 1891 – brings you to **The Turk's Head** 18 on the corner of Tench St. Return to Meeting House Alley and continue north to Watts Street, where, on the corner opposite Wapping Green, is **Turner's Old Star** 19, a traditional East End pub reportedly once owned by artist J.M.W. Turner. Carry on ahead to Chandler Street and turn right, then left on Wapping Lane. On the right are Raines Mansions' gardens and, next door, **Raine's House** 20 (Grade I listed), built in 1719 as a charity school by Henry Raine (1679-1738).

Wapping Lane continues north, crossing the **Ornamental Canal** 21, which runs through the heart of Wapping from the Hermitage Waterside development in the west to Shadwell Basin in the east. On the left just past the canal is historic **Tobacco Dock** 22 (see box), one of Wapping's best-preserved warehouses. Just over The Highway at

---

Tobacco Dock

Constructed in 1811, Tobacco Dock (Grade I listed, tobaccodocklondon.com) is a former brick-built tobacco warehouse with vaults, stunning timber beams, fine ironwork, and indoor and outdoor courtyards – now an events' space. At the dock's northern entrance is a 7ft (2.1m) bronze sculpture of a boy and a tiger. It commemorates an incident in 1857, when Charles Jamrach, a dealer in exotic animals, saved a young boy from the jaws of an escaped Bengal tiger. At the southern end of the dock are two replica pirate ships, *Sea Lark* and *Three Sisters* – built to house a museum and entertain children – the legacy of an ill-fated attempt to create a shopping centre in 1989.

Just before the Met's Marine Policing Unit is **Waterside Gardens** 15, overlooking the Thames, while opposite is the entrance to **Wapping Rose Gardens**

Ornamental Canal

St George-in-the-East

Ventilation shaft

the end of Wapping Lane is **St George-in-the-East** 23 (Grade I listed), a beautiful Anglican church designed by Nicholas Hawksmoor and constructed 1714-1729. Return to the canal and walk east along the waterway, through Wapping Woods and across Garnet Street to **Shadwell Basin** 24. Once linked to the Eastern Dock, this 7-acre (2.8ha) basin is one of the largest bodies of water to survive from London Docklands.

Prospect of Whitby

Turn left to walk clockwise around the basin. On the north side, behind Shadwell Terrace, is **St Paul's Shadwell** 25 which dates from 1821. It's known as the 'church of the sea captains', as it's said that 75 sea captains are buried here. Continue along the path and at the end go right on Wapping Wall – over the red swing bridge guarding Shadwell Basin – to visit another famous pub, the **Prospect of Whitby** 26. Built around 1520 (when it was called the Devil's Tavern), it's claimed to be London's oldest riverside inn, although the current building dates from the 19th

century. Near the shoreline is an eye-catching hangman's gibbet and noose – a grim reminder of Execution Dock.

Return to Wapping Wall and after re-crossing the red swing bridge pick up the Thames Path on the right, which runs along the southern perimeter of **King Edward VII Memorial Park** 27 (8 acres/3.3ha), opened in 1922 in memory of the late king. The path passes a circular red-brick building which is a **Ventilation Shaft** 28 for the Rotherhithe Tunnel (A101) running beneath the park and on to Rotherhithe on the southern bank of the Thames (see **Walk 16**). Continue along the Thames, where you pass some striking red-brick flats (the Free Trade Wharf development) and converted Georgian wharf buildings once owned by the East India Company. After a few hundred metres the path turns inland to join historic Narrow Street in Limehouse – so called because of the lime kilns that once stood here – which is lined with converted warehouses along the riverfront. The entrance to Rotherhithe

The Narrow

Tunnel is just north of here and beyond is **The Royal Foundation of St Katharine** ㉙ – the successor to Queen Matilda's hospital of St Katharine by the Tower – now a modern religious retreat and conference centre.

Limehouse Cut

A straight, broad canal (2 miles/3.2km) linking the lower reaches of the River Lea at Bow Creek/Bow Locks to the River Thames at Limehouse, the Limehouse Cut opened in 1769. In 1854 the Regent's Canal took control of the Cut and built a connecting link into the Regent's Canal Dock, now called the Limehouse Basin.

A short way along Narrow Street you pass **La Figa** ㉚, a stylish Italian restaurant, opposite which is a narrow alleyway leading back to the Thames Path. Turn left along the river to Gordon Ramsay's gastropub, **The Narrow** ㉛, on the corner of **Limehouse Ship Lock** ㉜. The upmarket pub occupies the old dock master's house and is a nice spot for lunch. From the pub go up the stairs and cross over Narrow Street Bridge – a swing bridge that swivels sideways to allow vessels to pass through the lock – and follow the path running alongside the right side of the lock to **Limehouse Basin** ㉝. Now a marina, the basin connects the River Lea (via Limehouse Cut) and the Regent's Canal with the Thames. From here you can see Canary Wharf, less than a kilometre away.

Follow the path around to the right to **Limehouse Cut** ㉞ (see box) and **Ropemakers Field** ㉟, where high-quality rope for marine anchors, rigging and mining was made for many centuries. Continue along the Cut towpath, and soon after you pass under the railway there are steps up to Newell Street. Turn left here to see the old **Limehouse Town Hall** ㊱ (built 1879-81), while just opposite the steps – along St Anne's Passage – is splendid Grade I listed **St Anne's Church** ㊲, designed by Nicholas Hawksmoor and consecrated in 1730. The church's prominent tower with its golden ball on a flagpole was designated a Trinity House 'sea mark' on navigational charts by Queen Anne, which permits the church to permanently display the White Ensign.

St Anne's Church

Return to Limehouse Cut and after 500m you pass **Bartlett Park** ㊳, with the shell of St Saviour's Church at its centre (destroyed by fire in 2007). Near its end the waterway goes under the A12 road and wends its way north to join the River Lea at **Bow Locks** ㊴, built in 1850 to link the tidal **Bow Creek** ㊵ to the Lee Navigation. Cross over the locks and

Limehouse Basin

House Mill Museum

The museum is housed in the magnificent House Mill (Grade I listed), the largest tidal mill still in existence in the world. Constructed in 1776 by Daniel Bisson, the mill trapped sea and river water at high tide, and the out-flowing water turned four huge water wheels, which in turn drove 12 pairs of millstones (the mechanism still survives, along with other historic machinery). In addition to flour-making, the mills prepared grain for a (gin) distillery based in Clerkenwell. House Mill ceased operation in 1941 after the area was bombed during the Second World War and was threatened with demolition in the mid-'70s. Restoration began in 1989, including the former Miller's House next door, which is now a visitor centre and café. For information and opening hours, see housemill.org.uk.

follow the path on the spit of land between the River Lea (on the left) and Bow Creek (on the right) to the end, where the path meets Three Mill Lane. Turn right to see the **House Mill Museum** **41** (see box) and Three Mills Island.

From the House Mill, go west along Three Mill Lane to the end, turn left on Hancock Road and cross under the busy A12 road via the subway opposite Tesco. The subway surfaces on the western side of the A12, where you walk south to St Leonard's Street and follow the path running alongside the A12 to Bromley-By-Bow tube station – and the end of the walk.

Three Mills Island

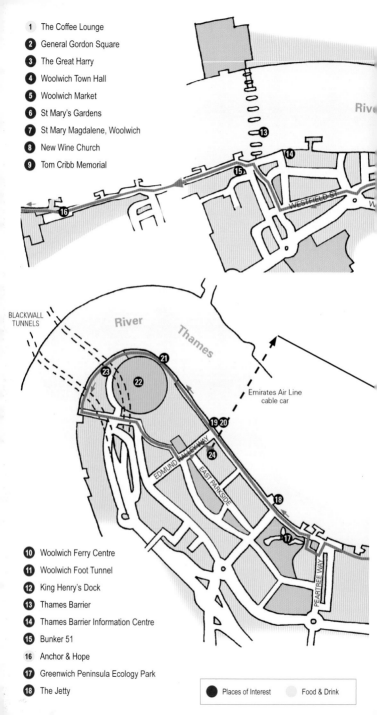

1. The Coffee Lounge
2. General Gordon Square
3. The Great Harry
4. Woolwich Town Hall
5. Woolwich Market
6. St Mary's Gardens
7. St Mary Magdalene, Woolwich
8. New Wine Church
9. Tom Cribb Memorial

River

WESTFIELD ST

BLACKWALL
TUNNELS

River Thames

Emirates Air Line
cable car

EDMUND HALLEY WAY

EAST PARKSIDE

PEARTREE WAY

10. Woolwich Ferry Centre
11. Woolwich Foot Tunnel
12. King Henry's Dock
13. Thames Barrier
14. Thames Barrier Information Centre
15. Bunker 51
16. Anchor & Hope
17. Greenwich Peninsula Ecology Park
18. The Jetty

Places of Interest   Food & Drink

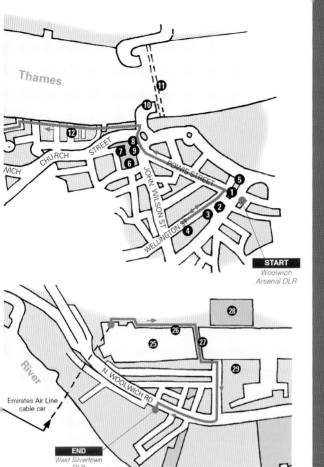

19 North Greenwich Pier

20 Quantum Cloud

21 Liberty Grip

22 O$_2$ Arena

23 A Slice of Reality

24 Emirates Greenwich Peninsula

25 Royal Victoria Dock

26 Sunborn London

27 Royal Victoria Bridge

28 Excel Exhibition Centre

29 Millennium Mills

Woolwich to Royal Victoria Dock

Distance: 6½ miles (10½ km)
Terrain: easy
Duration: 3 hours
Start: Woolwich Arsenal DLR
End: West Silvertown DLR
Postcode: SE18 6EU

Originally in Kent but now part of southeast London, Woolwich became a Metropolitan Borough in 1889 and part of the borough of Greenwich in 1965. Woolwich – the name derives from an Anglo-Saxon word meaning a 'trading place for wool' – is believed to have been inhabited since at least the Iron Age, and the Romans built a fort here. It remained a relatively small Kentish settlement until the 16th century, when it began to develop into a maritime, military and industrial centre.

In 1512, Henry VIII established a Royal Dockyard in Woolwich (which closed in 1869). A rope-making facility soon followed, as did the Woolwich Warren (1671) and the Royal Laboratory (1695), where explosives, fuses, shot and the like were produced. The complex of factories was renamed the Royal Arsenal in 1805 and it remained the largest munitions producer in the country until well into the 20th century. After closing in 1967 Woolwich went into sharp decline, although it has subsequently been regenerated.

Further west along the Thames, the Greenwich Peninsula has been transformed from an industrial wasteland into one of southeast London's most dynamic districts with a plethora of new homes and leisure facilities, while just a short cable car (or tube/boat) ride away is the revived Royal Docks area, home to the Excel Exhibition Centre and London City Airport.

The walk begins in Woolwich town centre and takes in the historic riverfront area before heading west along the Thames Path, via King Henry's Dock, to the Thames Barrier. From the Barrier we continue to North Greenwich and the magnificent O₂ Arena, before taking the Emirates Air Line cable car to the Royal Docks, ending the walk in Silvertown.

Greenwich Peninsula

Start Walking...

Exiting Woolwich Arsenal DLR station onto Beresford Square, turn left and walk towards Greens End. On the left-hand corner is **The Coffee Lounge 1**, perfect for a caffeine fix. Continue along the top of **General Gordon Square 2** – named after General Charles George Gordon (1833-1885), aka 'Gordon of Khartoum', who was born in Woolwich – to Wellington Street. On the left is **The Great Harry 3**, a Wetherspoon's pub named after Henry VIII's flagship *Henry Grace à Dieu* (Henry Grace of God, commonly known as Great Harry), which was built in Woolwich 1512-14. If you need more than coffee, the Harry serves breakfast until noon. Around 100m up on your right is handsome **Woolwich Town Hall 4** (Grade II* listed, see box); don't miss the chance to peek inside.

Retrace your steps to Beresford Square, the venue for **Woolwich Market 5** – a council-run market with its origins in the 17th-century (Mon-Wed 9am-4pm, Thu 9am-1pm, Fri-Sat 9am-4.30pm, Sun 10am-4.30pm – see woolwichmarket. com). Opposite the DLR station is Powis Street, Woolwich's late 18th-century main shopping street, named after the Powis brothers (Greenwich brewers) who developed it. Although rebuilt a number of times and full of 21st-century chain stores, the street still has some notable examples of late-Victorian and Art Deco architecture.

Walk to the end of Powis Street – just under 1km (0.5mi) – and cross John Wilson Street to **St Mary's Gardens 6** and **St Mary Magdalene, Woolwich 7** church. The gardens – now a

Woolwich Town Hall

The grand home of Greenwich Borough Council, Woolwich Town Hall was designed by Sir Alfred Brumwell Thomas in Baroque Revival style and opened in 1906 as the seat of the Metropolitan Borough of Woolwich. Now Grade II* listed, the building has two imposing monumental façades, along Wellington and Market Streets, with a 131ft (40m) Italianate tower on the corner. However, its crowning glory is the magnificent Victoria Hall, with its beautiful stained glass windows, portraits and monuments.

public park – are the former churchyard, designed in the English landscape style in 1893 by Fanny Wilkinson, Britain's first professional female landscape gardener. The current church was built 1732-1739 and due to its past importance as a navigation point for river traffic, it's entitled to fly the Red Ensign flag on ceremonial occasions. In the northeast corner of the gardens is the **New Wine Church 8**, a vast non-denominational Christian church occupying the former Art Deco

Woolwich Market

Coronet Cinema (1937). In the churchyard behind the old cinema is the tomb of world champion bare-knuckle boxer **Tom Cribb 9** (1781-1848), who was born in Woolwich; it features an unusual Coade stone monument of a lioness resting a paw on an urn.

Over the roundabout is the **Woolwich Ferry Centre 10** (see box) which links Woolwich with North Woolwich on the opposite bank of the Thames. Just east of the ferry approach is the Waterfront Leisure Centre and tucked in front of it is an unusual circular brick building: the entrance to the **Woolwich Foot Tunnel 11**. The tunnel was designed by Sir Maurice Fitzmaurice and opened in 1912, offering pedestrians and cyclists an alternative – if slightly claustrophobic – route across the river. It's 1,654ft (504m) by foot, emerging just east of the ferry terminal. From here, head west on the

Food & Drink

1 The Coffee Lounge: Handy café close to Woolwich Arsenal DLR station (Mon-Fri 6.30am-6pm, Sat 8am-6pm, Sun 9am-6pm, £).

16 Anchor & Hope: Traditional pub overlooking the Thames, serving fine ales and inexpensive pub grub (11am-11pm, £).

22 O$_2$ Arena: The O$_2$ contains a plethora of cafés and restaurants to suit every taste and pocket (most eateries open around 10.30/11am and close at 10.30/11pm, £-££).

Thames Path, where around 200m along is **King Henry's Dock 12**, where Henry VIII's ships were moored. The two docks are now surrounded by modern housing, but the long river frontage provides spectacular views.

Woolwich Ferry

There's been a ferry service across the Thames at Woolwich since at least the 14th century, although the 'current' Woolwich Ferry began operating in 1889. Unusually for London, the ferry is free, and carries around 2 million passengers annually – pedestrians, cyclists, cars, vans and lorries – connecting London's orbital North Circular and South Circular roads. The ferry operates every 5-10 minutes throughout the day, from Monday to Friday (6.10am-8pm) and every 15 minutes on Saturdays/public holidays (6.10am-8pm) and Sundays (11.30am-7.30pm).

King Henry's Dock

Keep walking west for around 250m, until the path turns away from the Thames, shown by a 'Thames Path' sign. This brings you out on Harlinger Street, where you turn right and then left on Ruston Road. Turn right at the T-junction, opposite a blackened building (a remnant of the Woolwich Dockyard), and after 250m go right at the roundabout to Warspite Road and left along Westfield Street. Near the end, where it becomes Eastmoor Place, turn right and follow the road and path along the edge of the park to Unity Way. Follow the road around to the right and cut left towards the river. From the waterfront there's an excellent view of the **Thames Barrier**  (see box) on your left; go right for the **Thames Barrier Information Centre** 14 (fee) and its View Café (Thu-Sun 10.30/11am-3/4pm depending on the time of year – see gov.uk/guidance/the-thames-barrier#visiting-the-thames-barrier for opening times).

Continue west along the Thames Path where a short way along is **Bunker 51** 15 , a decommissioned cold war nuclear bunker that's now a state-of-the-art centre for paintball and laser tag gaming. Around 400m further on you come to the **Anchor & Hope** 16 pub on the Riverside in Charlton, with a terrace overlooking the Thames (one of the few options for lunch before you reach the O₂ Arena). Continue

> ### Thames Barrier
>
> One of the world's largest movable flood barriers, the Thames Barrier spans 1,700ft (520m) and protects 48mi² (124km²) of central London from flooding caused by tidal surges. It was officially opened in 1984 and consists of ten movable steel gates – each weighing 3,300 tonnes – which stand as high as a five-storey building when raised. The attractive sculptural gates are like vast metallic sails or shells (or even shiny armadillos, according to some people), and look particularly elegant in strong sunshine or at dusk when the Barrier is floodlit.

Greenwich Peninsula Ecology Park

along the Thames Path, which turns briefly inland around the Greenwich Yacht Club and brings you to the **Greenwich Peninsula Ecology Park** 17 (Wed-Sun 10am-5pm/dusk in winter). Created in the '90s, the 4-acre (1.6ha) park is a little-known gem, comprising marshland,

Thames Barrier

A Slice of Reality

two lakes, streams, wetland, woodland and a meadow, where wildlife thrives.

Back on the Thames Path – here dubbed the Olympian Way – you pass towering blocks of flats on the regenerated Greenwich Peninsula and **The Jetty** ⓲ on the right, which hosts eclectic events and riverside gardening for the community. Around 400m further on the cables overhead lead to the Emirates Greenwich Peninsula over on the left – the Greenwich terminal for the Emirates Air Line cable car, which you experience later. A little further along, just before the **North Greenwich Pier** ⓳ – served by river boat services operated by Thames Clippers – is Anthony Gormley's (2000) **Quantum Cloud** ⓴, a massive 98ft (30m) sculpture made from 5-foot long sections of steel, incorporating around 3.5 miles (5.6km) of steel and weighing some 50 tonnes. It's one of several sculptures which make up the Greenwich Peninsula Sculpture Trail (see the-line.org). A few hundred metres further along on Olympian Way is another sculpture, **Liberty Grip** ㉑ by Gary Hume (2008), an abstract bronze.

The sculpture stands in the shadow of the **O₂ Arena** ㉒ (see box), a major London landmark.

O₂ Arena

The O₂ Arena is part of the reinvention of the iconic Millennium Dome, designed by Richard Rogers and built to house an exhibition celebrating the turn of the third millennium in 2000. It was renamed the O₂ in 2005 and redeveloped as an entertainment centre, including an indoor arena – the O₂ Arena – music club, cinema, exhibition space, piazzas, bars and restaurants. The 23,000-capacity O₂ Arena was the first purpose-built music venue in London and is also an important centre for sports events. If you're peckish, the O₂ contains a huge choice of restaurants.

Continue along the path around the top of the peninsula, where you see **A Slice of Reality** ㉓, an art installation by Richard Wilson (2000), comprising a 66ft (20m) high cross-section of an ocean-going sea dredger (the *Arco Trent*) mounted on the riverbed. From the installation continue south along the Olympian Way, where after around 300m the path turns inland and joins Waterview Drive just past the Intercontinental Hotel. After 400m you come to a roundabout where you go right (south) on Millennium Way past North Greenwich tube station and turn left along

Royal Victoria Dock

Edmund Halley Way. Towards the end, on the right, is the **Emirates Greenwich Peninsula** 24 , the terminal of the Emirates Air Line cable car between Greenwich Peninsula and the Royal Victoria Dock. Board the cable car and around 5 minutes later (the trip takes 12-13 minutes after 7pm) you arrive at the **Royal Victoria Dock** 25 on the north side of the Thames. The largest of three docks that comprised the Royal Docks (see box), now part of the redeveloped Docklands, the Royal Victoria Dock was designed by George Parker Bidder and opened in 1855. The dock is still accessible to ships, although its western entrance has been in-filled and is now mainly used for water sports.

From the Emirates Air Line terminal, walk east along the perimeter of the dock passing the **Sunborn London** 26 , a Finnish-built yacht that's now a luxury hotel ship. Just past the yacht is the **Royal Victoria Bridge** 27 – a footbridge completed in 1998 and positioned high so

Royal Docks

The Royal Docks (not to be confused with the Royal Dockyards) comprised the Royal Albert Dock, the Royal Victoria Dock and the King George V Dock, completed between 1855 and 1921. Collectively they formed the largest enclosed docks in the world, with a water area of almost 250 acres (101ha) and an overall area of 1,100 acres (445ha). The docks closed in 1981 and were redeveloped in the '80s and '90s.

imposing **Millennium Mills** 29 , a former flour mill built in the '30s, now being reinvented as a business centre, while in the distance to the east is City Airport, London's fifth-largest international airport handling some five million passengers a year.

Continue south on Rayleigh Road into Mill Road and go right on North Woolwich Road to West Silvertown railway station/ DLR – and the end of the walk.

Emirates Greenwich Peninsula cable car

as not to impede yachts passing below – and beyond it, the **Excel Exhibition Centre** 28 , a vast (100-acre/40ha) exhibition and international convention centre opened in 2000. Cross the bridge to the south side and go left along the path to Rayleigh Road. On the immediate left is the

Royal Victoria Bridge

London's Architectural Walks

ISBN: 978-1-909282-85-8, 128 pages, softback, £9.99, Jim Watson

London's Architectural Walks is a unique guide to the most celebrated landmark buildings in one of the world's major cities. In thirteen easy walks, it takes you on a fascinating journey through London's diverse architectural heritage with historical background and clear maps. Some of the capital's most beautiful parks are visited, plus palaces, theatres, museums and some surprising oddities.

The author's line and watercolour illustrations of all the city's significant buildings, make London's Architectural Walks an essential companion for anyone interested in the architecture that has shaped this great metropolis.

London's Secret Walks, 3rd Edition

ISBN: 978-1-909282-99-5, 320 pages, softback, £10.99
David Hampshire

London is a great city for walking – whether for pleasure, exercise or simply to get from A to B. Despite the city's extensive public transport system, walking is often the quickest and most enjoyable way to get around – at least in the centre – and it's also free and healthy! Many attractions are off the beaten track, away from the major thoroughfares and public transport hubs. This favours walking as the best way to explore them, as does the fact that London is a visually interesting city with a wealth of stimulating sights in every 'nook and cranny'.

Touring the Cotswolds

ISBN: 978-1-909282-91-9, 128 pages, softback, £9.99, Jim Watson

Touring the Cotswolds is a unique guide to exploring the best of the Cotswolds by car through eight carefully planned tours that take in the heavyweight tourist centres plus a wealth of hidden gems (the 'real Cotswolds'). You'll negotiate a maze of country lanes, high hills with panoramic views, lush woodlands and beautiful valleys, plus an abundance of picturesque villages, providing a comprehensive portrait of this varied and delightful area.

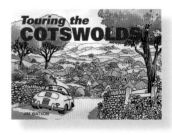

INDEX

W

Y

London's Green Walks

ISBN: 978-1-909282-82-7, 192 pages, £9.99
David Hampshire

Green spaces cover almost 40 per cent of Greater London, ranging from magnificent royal parks and garden cemeteries, full of intrigue and history, to majestic ancient forests and barely tamed heathland; from elegant squares and formal country parks to enchanting 'secret' gardens. The 20 walks take in famous destinations, such as Hyde Park and Regent's Park, but also many smaller and lesser known – but no less beautiful – parks and gardens, all of which are free to explore.

London's Village Walks

ISBN: 978-1-909282-94-0, 192 pages, £9.99
David Hampshire

From its beginnings as a Roman trading port some 2,000 years ago, London has mushroomed into the metropolis we see today, swallowing up thousands of villages, hamlets and settlements in the process. Nevertheless, if you're seeking a village vibe you can still find it if you know where to look. Scratch beneath the surface of modern London and you'll find a rich tapestry of ancient villages, just waiting to be rediscovered.

London's Monumental Walks

ISBN: 978-1-909282-95-7, 192 pages, £9.99
David Hampshire

It isn't perhaps surprising that in a city as rich in history as London, there's a wealth of public monuments, statues and memorials: in fact London probably has more statues than any other world city. Its streets, squares, parks and gardens are crammed with monuments to kings and queens, military heroes, politicians and local worthies, artists and writers, and notables from every walk of life (plus a few that commemorate deeds and people best forgotten), along with a wealth of abstract and contemporary works of art.

Peaceful London, 2nd edition

ISBN: 978-1-909282-84-1, 192 pages, softback, £9.99
David Hampshire

Whether you're seeking a place to recharge your batteries, rest your head, revive your spirits, restock your larder or refuel your body; somewhere to inspire, soothe or uplift your mood; or just wish to discover a part of London that's a few steps further off the beaten track, *Peaceful London* will steer you in the right direction.

Quirky London, 2nd edition

ISBN: 978-1-909282-98-8, 192 pages, softback, £9.99
David Hampshire, published Summer 2019

The British are noted for their eccentricities and London is no exception, with an abundance of bizarre and curious places and stories. *Quirky London* explores over 300 of the city's more unusual places and sights that often fail to register on the radar of both visitors and residents alike.

London Escapes

ISBN: 978-1-913171-00-1, 192 pages, softback, £9.99
David Hampshire, published Autumn 2019

London offers a wealth of attractions, but sometimes you just want to escape the city's constant hustle and bustle and visit somewhere with a gentler, slower pace of life. *London Escapes* offers over 70 days out, from historical towns and lovely villages to magnificent stately homes and gardens; beautiful, nostalgic seaside resorts and beaches to spectacular parks and nature reserves.